Creating a Culture of Invitation
in Your Church

By the same author

*Unlocking the Growth*

# Creating
# a Culture of
# Invitation
# in Your Church

## MICHAEL HARVEY

MONARCH
BOOKS

Oxford UK, and Grand Rapids, USA

Published by Monarch Books
an imprint of
**Lion Hudson plc**
Wilkinson House, Jordan Hill Road,
Oxford OX2 8DR, England
Email: monarch@lionhudson.com
www.lionhudson.com/monarch

ISBN 978 0 85721 632 8
e-ISBN 978 0 85721 633 5

First edition 2015

**Acknowledgments**
Unless otherwise stated Scripture quotations taken from the Holy Bible, New International
Version Anglicised. Copyright © 1979, 1984, 2011 Biblica, formerly International Bible
Society. Used by permission of Hodder & Stoughton Ltd, an Hachette UK company. All
rights reserved. "NIV" is a registered trademark of Biblica. UK trademark number 1448790.
Scripture quotations marked ESV are from The Holy Bible, English Standard Version® (ESV®)
copyright © 2001 by Crossway, a publishing ministry of Good News Publishers. All rights
reserved.
Scripture marked NASB taken from the New American Standard Bible®, Copyright © 1960,
1962, 1963, 1968, 1971, 1972, 1973, 1975, 1977, 1995 by The Lockman Foundation. Used
by permission.
Scripture marked NKJV taken from the New King James Version. Copyright © 1982 by
Thomas Nelson, Inc. Used by permission. All right reserved.
Scripture taken from The Message. Copyright © by Eugene H. Peterson 1993, 1994, 1995,
1996, 2000, 2001, 2002. Used by permission of NavPress Publishing Group.

A catalogue record for this book is available from the British Library

Printed and bound in the UK, June 2015, LH26

*In memory of Frank and Anne Perrott*
*and to my incredible wife Eike,*
*and children Ben, Kirsty and Lydia*

# Contents

# Acknowledgments

I am blessed to have a mum who invited me and a grandma who supported my attendance at Church.

I am indebted to Frank and Anne Perrott, who blessed me with their friendship and advice from eleven years of age and accompanied me through four decades of life.

I acknowledge Lightbowne Evangelical Church, who are a true sending church, taking those who the world would reject and seeing transformed lives.

Thanks to the Back to Church Sunday Team, who have created the Season of Invitation for friendship and support.

In recent years God has blessed me with the friendship and advice of David Pitts, John Cavanagh, and Greg Murray, who have all contributed to this book by offering a listening ear and not being afraid to correct my many wanderings.

I thank Tony Collins and the team at Monarch, especially Richard Herkes and Sheila Jacobs.

I thank all the church leaders who have had to put up with me inviting them into a conversation, especially those who said no. For it was through the no that I learnt the most.

For those congregational members who have tried to invite and whether you have got a yes or no, I want to say well done, good and faithful servant.

To my children Ben, Kirsty, and Lydia, know that I am really proud of you.

Finally my beautiful wife Eike, who allows me to wander the world as an itinerant provoker. She says to all who listen, my short absence gives her a break!

# Foreword

I've worked with Michael Harvey for almost ten years. In each one of those years I've seen what a disciplined, passionate love for God's church can do, as Michael has brought his ideas, experience and skill to bear on the moment of invitation.

Evangelism is not difficult, but it can be hard. Both for individual Christians and for churches, the call of God is to overcome fear and to grow in confidence. I know of no one who has explored these matters, and who has resourced the Church in this area, more wisely than Michael.

His book cuts to the heart of the evangelism conundrum. It's so simple to say to our friends, "I'm a Christian", or to say "Would you like to come to church with me?" Simple, but not easy. We know exactly what we need to do, but somehow when the moment of invitation comes, we let it go by. This book focuses in on the reasons why we find it hard to share our faith or to invite our friends, and with unerring humour and lightness of touch it skewers the rationalizations and the "sophisticated" reasons we invent to get away from the moment.

Reading the book, you meet Michael. For the thousands who have already met him in his "Unlocking the Growth" seminars, the book will bring back a smile or a nod as we hear his voice again and agree with its common sense. If you've not yet met him, the book will open a door into the research, analysis, passion, and prayer that have made his work so valuable to us all.

"My friend is rather shy, but she formed a bridge and Jesus Christ walked over it." That's evangelism. You may want to form a bridge, to help your church form bridges, so that Jesus Christ can walk across to the people you know and love. If you want that, read this book.

*Paul Bayes is Anglican Bishop of Liverpool, and a member of the leadership team for the Season of Invitation.*

# Preface

This book was born in 1971 when an eight-year-old boy was invited to a church much closer to home than the one that took a two-mile walk every Sunday. Where would that boy be without that invitation? I am that boy, and this book is another step along the path of my healing. It was at that church in north Manchester that I met my spiritual father, Frank Perrott, who invited me into the life of the church and to a faith in Jesus Christ.

Between 1963 and 1971, my formative years, I didn't live with my mum, I never knew my father, a sibling was born and taken away without my knowledge, I had a skin colour that was different from those at school, and I had my original name removed. These events became the window through which I viewed the world – and to some extent, they still are.

Frank was later joined by his wife, Anne, in helping me to discover a relationship with God. They were both a vital presence during my teenage years, as I spent time with others in the youth group in their home. Together with other people at the church, they encouraged the transformation of the life of a boy hurt by his past. They wept alongside me as I saw my mum die early and my grandmother develop Alzheimer's. At that difficult time I swapped roles with my grandma and became her carer. Later on, Anne and Frank rejoiced with me as I married and had a family of my own. They both felt pride as they saw me succeed in business, and then were amazed and delighted as I started to take a message of invitation first around the UK and then around the world. Their faith was inspirational, and without their constant invitation to take a closer look at Jesus Christ, I am not sure where I would be today.

I wept with Frank as his precious wife died. And I wept again as Frank died even as a new life was starting for him. In a way, Frank had carried me into the church through his friendship, and I now had the privilege of carrying him back into church for his final earthly journey.

I dedicate this book to the memory of Anne and Frank Perrott. But it takes a whole church to raise an inviter for Christ.

# Introduction

Take a moment to thank God for the person who invited you to take a closer look at Jesus Christ. It might have been an event, a church service, or simply to a cup of coffee… but they invited you.

I want to start a process that leads to change. As I have travelled the world in the last ten years, increasingly I have tried to understand why Christians have such difficulty in reaching out to friends and neighbours through the simple act of invitation.

This is a book born in pain. My pain stems from the fact that I have spent ten years fighting for attention. I have had to travel thousands of miles to speak for fifteen minutes. When I have reached an important part in talking about my research, I have been cut off because time has gone, and another meeting calls. We are all just so very busy. We have created unceasing endeavours to divert ourselves.

While many of my ideas may sound familiar, they cut across an aspect of church life which might best be described as "business as usual". The ideas I promote might be "lovely", but we have a church to run and maintain, services to plan, rotas to fill, systems to keep going, and people to pay. Therefore the question I hear the most from church leaders is: "Does it work?"

If it is too hard for clergy, they tend to go quiet, change the subject afterwards, and get back onto much safer territory. There are very few questions afterwards, polite and blank looks with very little engagement. These are the hardest audiences, not because they challenge what I say but because they don't know what to do with it.

Then there is the criticism from some missional thinkers who have labelled Back to Church Sunday nothing more than an energetic attempt to get the lapsed to attend. They maintain that the attractional model of church is not based on "mission" and is going nowhere. In their otherwise excellent book *The Faith of Leap*,[1] Michael Frost and Alan Hirsch highlight an Anglican church that gave chocolate to those who accepted the invitation and go on to say that the church was thus "reduced to begging people to come" which they said is "not only pathetic but borders on false witness".

However, while there is pain, I have used the frustration and the space given by rejection to seek greater clarity in this area of mission. The frustration has proved very beneficial! It has helped to test and refine the calling, to gather ideas and embrace more innovation.

My hope is that the strategies in this book will be used to address the difficulties we face in our churches, and that this will lead to far more mission activity.

As we go into mission or pastoral work we might think that we are bringing God with us – as if previously God were somehow absent. Vincent Donovan, author of *Christianity Rediscovered*, says this:

> *God was there before we ever got there… it is simply up*
> *to us to bring him out*
> *so that they can recognise him.*[2]

We should be going into mission with confidence that we will find God as we go – and when we get there. This is the thrill of developing a culture of invitation.

I have conducted ten years' study of the art of invitation, over 650 times in twelve countries, and for the first ten years I asked just one question: "Why don't we invite our friends to take a closer look at Christ and his church?"

On all of those occasions no one ever told me that it was a stupid question. They just went on to tell me the reasons that were hindering them from invitation. Now, I am one of those people more fascinated when things go wrong than when they go right. In my first book, *Unlocking the Growth*, I made the case that we are locking down the growth that God wants to give to the church. We are in fact hiding a breakdown in our relationship with God. When we hide this and bury it deep within our thinking, we lose out. But there is hope. From sin comes salvation; from Good Friday comes Easter Sunday; from a breakdown in our relationship with God, transformation can come. When God turns up in many of our Bible stories it is to bring deliverance from disobedience. And so it is today.

So is anything hindering you and your church? Let me ask you a different question that might well expose why this book might be important for you. One question, but you're only allowed to choose one of the two options.

*Is your congregation welcoming or inviting?*

You can imagine the answer I receive to that question, can't you? "Welcoming." But how welcoming can we be if we are not inviting?

We are welcoming (well, some of us are) as long as people get themselves across the threshold of a church building. And this is where we so often fail, by not taking our welcome outside with a gift of an invitation. Whereas I have found that when Christians start to invite, we see people accepting (as well as rejecting) invitations in big numbers across the world.

Invitation is at the heart of God himself. He sent his Son to invite us all into a relationship. And so to be a person who invites is to be like God.

But there is a problem deep within in us, causing our reluctance. Consider the following verse quoted by Jesus from the prophet Isaiah:

> *The Spirit of the Sovereign Lord is on me, because the*
> *Lord has anointed me to proclaim good news to the*
> *poor. He has sent me to bind up the broken-hearted,*
> *to proclaim freedom for the captives and release from*
> *darkness for the prisoners (Isaiah 61:1)*

I find Christians who are unknowingly captive, bound up in fear and broken-hearted. But the great news is that Jesus came to set us free and heal the broken-hearted. Ralph Waldo Emerson discussed the potential in releasing the captives:

> *Everything in creation has its appointed painter or poet*
> *and remains in bondage like the princess in the fairy*
> *tale till its appropriate liberator comes to set it free.*[3]

But you cannot escape captivity if you don't know you are captive in the first place; you can't begin a healing process if you don't know your heart is broken. On the other hand, if Jesus has proclaimed freedom for the captives, why would you ever go back to prison when you are free?

There is a reason why. It is a fact that the unconscious habits of a lifetime don't just roll over and die when we become Christians. We have to appropriate the freedom that Christ proclaims, and mission gives us the opportunity to see our captivity and our broken-heartedness brought into the clear light of day.

I must declare an interest in this area of captivity and broken-heartedness, lest I "look at the speck of sawdust in [my] brother's eye and pay no attention to the plank in [my] own" (Matthew 7:3). I too find myself full of fear and hindered by a past which is still being healed and is not yet sorted. So I am addressing myself as well as you. It is the possibility of my own freedom and healing that makes this subject, for me, almost impossible to resist. I teach and research that which I need the most.

I write into a generation of church leadership that is puzzling to work out how to be effective in mission on one end of the spectrum, while on the other end it is trying simply to keep the doors of churches open by attracting newcomers. I am reminded of the question of the Ethiopian eunuch: "'How can I [understand],' he said, 'unless someone explains it to me?'" (Acts 8:31).

Now, if I could be considered a teacher, I am almost embarrassed to bring you uncommon sense, but here it is:

> *If we invite people, some will say no and some will say yes; but if we don't invite people, the answer will always be no!*

John Wooden, a legendary US sports coach, once said:

> *It's what you learn after you know it all that counts.*[4]

Truth is often hidden in clear sight.

So here is a formula for invitational mission in just three letters:

**a... s ... k**

Receiving is reserved for those who ask; finding for those who seek; and open doors for those who knock on a few! Experience of getting a negative response can be so overrated – especially when it keeps you from going on asking people.

Invitation to church may seem old hat to you. But sometimes blessing comes if we revisit some well-worn but forgotten spiritual principles. We need the fresh water of God's blessing.

> *Isaac reopened the wells that had been dug in the time of his father Abraham, which the Philistines had stopped up after Abraham died, and he gave them the same names his father had given them. (Genesis 26:18)*

Just as Isaac revisited and reopened the wells, I intend to re-look at some very old principles.

In chapter one we will look at where invitation is going wrong; in chapter two, the reasons we don't invite; in chapter three, how to face fear; in chapter four, responding to rejection; in chapter five, how to address the problem; in chapter six, best practice; and in chapter seven, who is the ultimate inviter.

# 1

## What's Wrong?

One example will suffice to underline a paradigm running in Western Christianity today. I ring a church leader after an event where the congregation has been encouraged to invite people along, and ask, "How did it go?" Then follows a variation on the following theme:

> *Church Leader: Terrible.*
>
> *Me: How do you mean, terrible?*
>
> *Church Leader: We only had ten invited guests.*
>
> *Me: That doesn't sound terrible.*
>
> *Church Leader: Yes, well, only one of them has stayed. So we're not doing another one of these events next year!*

Apparently we are not content with ones and twos, and we discount everything else in the process. I said in *Unlocking the Growth*[5] that I believe success isn't a percentage, a number, or a line on a graph; success is one person inviting one person. My findings show that whatever we say, we still really believe that success is one person inviting one person *and that person saying yes*.

To counter this success thinking, I want to remind you of what Jesus said in the parable of the talents: "You have been faithful with a few things; I will put you in charge of many things" (Matthew 25:21). Faithfulness should be our main concern. Results are God's concern.

I would say that it is hard enough for a congregation member to invite without the added pressure of having to get a yes. This pressure to succeed actually cuts off invitation, because the common defence in avoiding the possibility of failure is to stop trying. Lower your expectations until they're already met, and you'll never be disappointed.

The heavy pressure to be successful can be replaced by the lightness of faithfulness, even when that includes what looks like failure. I believe the greatest way to change another person's behaviour is to change their paradigm – change the map of how they see themselves, their role, and their responsibility. So if you remember nothing else in this book, please remember this:

> *Success is one person inviting one person, leaving the*
> *yes and the no to God.*

Even the great apostle Paul said:

> *I planted the seed, Apollos watered it, but God has been*
> *making it grow. (1 Corinthians 3:6)*

Will someone say yes, or no? The fact is, you cannot plan the impact that you will have. In fact, you won't even recognize it when it is happening. You certainly will make an impact, but you will probably never know what it is.

Research professor at the University of Houston, Brené Brown says:

> *We have lost our ability to be uncertain.*[6]

It seems that these days, before we do anything, we need to remove all risk of uncertainty and failure. As a result we don't actually use our faith. Faith which goes into uncertain situations has gone out of fashion, exchanged for certainty.

Now, that does not mean that we are going into mission as a completely disinterested party. We go into mission with hope. Hope contains both trust and distrust in tension. Hope is the confident expectation of something desired in the face of the possibility that it may not happen. But our Christian hope brings a belief that good will come even in the face of things that look bad. The difference between the two is crucial. Do we have hope that in every difficulty lies an opportunity?

By contrast many of us in the church measure our self-worth according to results rather than efforts. We then put in less effort – which produces less by way of results! As the saying goes:

> *If at first you don't succeed… hide all evidence that you tried!*

The success paradigm has developed in the church through distorted truth. We hear ourselves saying about an event, or an initiative, "Did it work? Did it produce fruit?" Of course we strive to be the best for God; we want to see people come to a relationship with Christ, for that is best for them. But when we don't see people responding positively immediately, the feeling of failure creeps in. We don't see that God might have another agenda. Perhaps he wants to use this to produce the fruit of the Spirit within us, the inviters; perhaps he wants to bring to the surface wounds that need healing.

What is driving the push for success? It is one of the most enslaving parts of church life and it is plaguing our generation. You may even be questioning my sanity as you read this, wondering why I would even suggest that success is wrong. But I am interested in this almost manic "push" for success. Alain Botton sees it as part of our loss of belief in a world beyond this one. In *Status Anxiety*[7] he writes:

*When a belief in the next world is interpreted as a childish and scientifically impossible opiate, the pressure to succeed and fulfil oneself will inevitably be inflamed by the awareness that there is only a single and frighteningly brief opportunity to do so. Earthly achievements can no longer be seen as an overture to what one may realize in another world, they are the sum total of all one will ever be.*

So we have become a society where we mustn't fail and there is only one right answer. As Glynn Harrison says in *The Big Ego Trip*:[8]

*So trained by our culture we think in terms of being winners and losers.*

It is a fear of getting things wrong. We only like the word "yes" and regret hearing the word "no". But this is highly problematical in mission, because we are bound to hear people say the word "no" to us!

Fear of being wrong has another consequence for us: it closes us off to growth. A person who does not mind being wrong is continually detecting, processing, and correcting in any potentially negative situation. Things are allowed to develop. I think it is time for us to give up the desire to be perfect and concentrate on *becoming* who we are meant to be.

In my research I have been pointed towards attribution theory to help understand this pervading desire to succeed that stalks the church.

Attribution theory looks at how we attribute meaning to

others' behaviour, or our own. For example: we ask, is this person angry because they are bad-tempered, or because something bad has happened to them?

Let's apply this to persistence in mission in the face of failure. Do we lack persistence because we are weak, or because of the difficulty of the task? Rather than use guilt as a stick to beat people with, I suggest we promote the difficulty of the task before us. This, then, gives scope to develop the character of the participants, as attribution is now shifted from internal to external factors – and we acknowledge that it is for God, not us, to give the results.

Paul picks up on this dynamic:

> Not only so, but we also glory in our sufferings, because we know that suffering produces perseverance; perseverance, character; and character, hope. (Romans 5:3–4)

Paul found that inner healing hurts. In going from freedom to slavery, there is pain. He found it through a process of facing difficulty.

The example from the children of Israel:

> Remember how the Lord your God led you all the way in the wilderness these forty years, to humble and test you in order to know what was in your heart, whether or not you would keep his commands. (Deuteronomy 8:2)

So, as we promote the difficulty of the task, I think our slogan could be:

> Become an invitational church – not just for the yeses, but for what you become in the process.

Persistence is the field of proving. Jesus went to the wilderness to be tested, and in a similar way, so will you. Another slogan:

> No test, no testimony.

Until we are tested, we don't know what we are made of. It gives us a sense of who we are in Christ. Adversity is simply change that we haven't yet embraced.

On the day the church was born, the day of Pentecost, some made fun of the disciples. You can just imagine some of the believers saying this "just isn't working". That's when Peter stood up!

Peter and John were seized by the authorities and thrown into jail. You can imagine some believers saying this "just isn't working". But then Peter, filled with the Holy Spirit and courage, told the officials by what authority they spoke.

Persecution followed. Good men were dragged off, and the authorities put them in prison as well. You can imagine some of the believers saying this "just isn't working". But they were scattered as far as Phoenicia, Cyprus, and Antioch, taking the good news wherever they went.

They stood up when being mocked, they stood up when being jailed, and they stood up when being persecuted. Do you notice any difference in the church today?

Seth Godin, American entrepreneur, author, and social commentator, wrote a little book in 2007 called *The Dip.* [9] The book teaches you when to quit and when to stick.

The dip is a temporary setback that can be overcome with persistence. The trick is to recognize if you are in a situation that's worth pushing through, or one where it's worth quitting.

Within this idea I find one of the major ways that God tries to teach us. Even a cursory glance through the pages of the Bible pulls up some examples: Moses' forty years in exile; Joseph's years in prison; Nathan's traumatic challenge of David's adultery and murder; the disciples' abandonment of Jesus; Paul's times in prison.

It is in the dip (if we choose to listen) that God disciples and matures us. Sooner or later the act of invitation creates such a dip for most of us, as we face the rejection of a friend or family member. Multiply this across a whole congregation and we have a whole church going through the dip together. Some people – some churches – choose to take the easy way out by quitting and stopping invitation entirely...

... while others make a glorious discovery: at our lowest ebb God is there and wants to deepen his relationship with us.

There is, I believe, a journey of transformation: that when we seem to lose we can win. Below you will see a shape called a parabola. I believe it is the shape of discipleship. We all dream of a steady upward path of progress as followers of Christ, but when you look at those saints who have gone before us, discipleship looks like this:

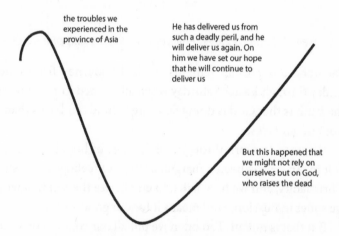

the troubles we experienced in the province of Asia

He has delivered us from such a deadly peril, and he will deliver us again. On him we have set our hope that he will continue to deliver us

But this happened that we might not rely on ourselves but on God, who raises the dead

We were under great pressure, far beyond our ability to endure so that we despaired of life itself. Indeed, we felt we had received the sentence of death

*(2 Corinthians 1:18; 2 Corinthians 1:10; 2 Corinthians 1:9; 2 Corinthians 1:8b–9a)*

It seems to me that transformation comes right in the midst of troubles. Here is another example:

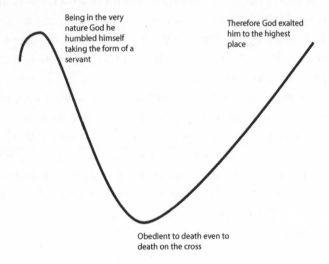

Being in the very nature God he humbled himself taking the form of a servant

Therefore God exalted him to the highest place

Obedient to death even to death on the cross

*(see Philippians 2:6–7, Philippians 2:9; see Philippians 2:8)*

Parabolic discipleship reminds us of the journey from Good Friday through Easter Saturday when all seemed lost, but where the truth is that God is doing far more behind our backs than in front of our faces.

We need to work through our feelings of hopelessness and failure. There has been a marginalization of feelings in Western Christianity, and we have failed to emphasize the fact that when we suffer in mission, God means it for our good.

But that is not all. Too often we put all our concern on to the people we are inviting, and forget about what is going on with the inviter. In my view, we are fishing on the wrong side of the boat! I am not going to disparage those who only concentrate on those we invite, but I think it is hopelessly narrow and leaves many inviters without the appropriate support. The inviter is utterly crucial to the invitation.

And that brings us to another challenge.

# 2

# Twelve Reasons for Not Inviting

At the time of writing I have conducted the same survey 700 times across thirteen countries. My one question: What are the reasons that we don't invite our friends?

I have found that between 80 per cent and 95 per cent of congregation members have no intention of inviting anyone. This is a surprise to most people. I have found it in growing churches also, where the percentage of intentional inviters might be 20 per cent compared with 5 per cent in non-growing churches. This still means that the vast majority of the congregation is not presently inviting and not about to start any time soon.

Here are the twelve common reasons why we do not invite, as outlined in my book *Unlocking the Growth*:

- I suffer, and I don't want my friend to suffer.
- My friend won't want to go as they said no to me last year.
- We have no non-churchgoing friends.
- It's the church leader's job.
- I was never invited – I was born into the church.
- What if it damages my friendship?

- Our services and people are unpredictable.
- I fear the congregation will think my friend is not "our" type of person.
- I am reticent.
- Religion is a private matter.
- I don't want to be seen as strange.
- They might ask something about my faith, and I wouldn't know what to say.

There is a point in my seminars when the light switches on, when each person suddenly becomes aware of the fear lurking in a corner of their mind; or they suddenly become conscious of the battle between faith and fear.

The first step towards change is awareness: we can't really change something until we are aware there is a problem. This is a major finding in my research:

*We are a church in fear, but we have very little perception of that fear.*

We are all at times unconsciously incompetent. We don't know what we don't know. Whereas, if we become aware, we acknowledge that incompetence, and this allows us to make the necessary change.

So let's look for the emotion lurking in those twelve answers.

## 1. I don't want my friend to suffer

One of the common reasons I hear for not being able to invite a friend is this: we can't invite them to our act of worship, as there is just no possibility they would get anything from it. *I suffer, and I don't want my friend to suffer.* But we all have examples of people being touched by God – yes, even when we felt there was no chance! Who would have said that Saul, chief persecutor of the early church, would find Christ?

Every church leader has known what it is to spend a week preparing their greatest sermon ever, only to be told afterwards that it was no more than "lovely" or "interesting". By the same token, that church leader can be totally without a clue all week about what to say, until throwing one together at the last moment, then to be told that the sermon really impacted people. Sometimes there is no apparent rhyme or reason to the activity of God. So why not take a chance that God will turn up?

## 2. My friend said no last year

This objection is equally common. It is a fact that our friends will say no to us at times. But we are too quick to let our "no" results control our thinking and action. A no result should not of itself stop us from considering a second shot at inviting people to take a closer look at Christ.

We can, of course, worry about the impact on our relationship, but perhaps we worry too much. In his book *The Lies We Tell Ourselves*,[10] Chris Thurman quotes the following humorous saying:

> *At age twenty, we worry about what others think of us.*
> *At forty, we don't care what they think of us. At sixty we*
> *discover they haven't been thinking about us at all.*

Thurman goes on to say:

> *People act the way they do because of who they are, not*
> *because of who we are. We can't afford to lose sight of*
> *that fact.*

Becoming invitational means undoubted rejection, humiliation, embarrassment, and pain. Maybe the ancient Franciscan prayer of discomfort might be helpful in pointing us towards the hidden benefits.

*May God bless you with discomfort at easy answers, half truths, and superficial relationships, so that you may live deep within your heart. May God bless you with anger at injustice, oppression, and exploitation of people, so that you may work for justice, freedom, and peace. May God bless you with tears to shed for those who suffer from pain, rejection, starvation, and war, so that you may reach out your hand to comfort them and to turn their pain into joy. May God bless you with enough foolishness to believe that you can make a difference in this world, so that you can do what others claim cannot be done. And the Blessing of God, who Creates, Redeems and Sanctifies, be upon you and all you love and pray for this day, and for ever.*

The fear of laughter of friends, neighbours, and work colleagues stops many an activity. To forgo popularity and stay on course despite the derision is a matter of grit and determination. They laughed at Alexander Bell about the telephone. They mocked Christopher Columbus, but did he fall off the earth? They said to Henry Ford: "Who needs a car? There are no roads anyway!" They derided Thomas Edison about the oil-less light bulb. They looked at the Wright Brothers and said, "It will never fly, Orville. Man was never meant to fly."

The vital characteristic these pioneers all showed was resilience – the ability to spring back after defeat, to ignore setbacks, disregard discouragement, rise above inevitable deterrents to action, and to combat the sheer inertia and indifference of others. Only a man or woman of vision will press on in the cause, in face of the apathy of others. The hunger of these men revealed stockpiles of reserves and energy. These reserves are called the second wind. But maybe we have a third wind, maybe even a tenth wind. The reserves lie dormant within us. That has certainly been my experience of introducing invitation into the life of the church. I still need today to disregard discouragement, and to help others who have been turned down once to try again and develop that second wind.

Another aspect of *My friend said no last year* is our own neediness. This can come into play when we are desperate for our friend or family member to accept an invitation. Here it is really important that we emotionally detach ourselves from the outcome – otherwise we are crippled if they say no. And in fact this investment of ourselves in the invitation can backfire, as our invitee senses it and pulls back. They have picked up our desperation for a yes. It is not important that they say yes, only that we offer the invitation; the rest we can leave to God. After all, our invitee might not be ready yet.

"They'll never come!" We are really good at making decisions on behalf of other people, but even more so when we have the unlikely candidate. This is the one who we just know is so anti anything to do with faith that we don't even bother. Perhaps they have vociferously said as much in the past, or we have been party to a conversation where they have derided Christ, so we leave them alone; this despite the fact that we gain a distinct impression that we should invite them to something.

Again, there are many examples of the unlikely candidate turning to Christ: the murderous Saul who became the apostle Paul; more recently, gang leader Nicky Cruz and atheistic scientist Francis Collins.

## 3. We have no non-churchgoing friends

This could indeed be true, or it might not be true and what they are really saying is, "You're not asking me to invite people I *know*, are you?" (Look of fear in the eyes.)

Let's say for a moment that we have a whole congregation that genuinely has no non-Christian friends. Surely that would lead a church leadership to wonder how we have allowed ourselves to become so ghettoized. That alone should lead to moving from an inward-looking to an outward focus.

And if it is not true that we have no non-Christian friends, then we are lying to ourselves.

## 4. It's the church leader's job

There is some truth in this. But it is clear to me, from touring some of the larger growing churches around the world, that congregations can often "hire away their responsibility". Nor is this exclusively a large church problem. We can all get into the mode of having other people lead our Christian lives for us. We can be cash-rich but time-poor, because of our jobs or the pull of retirement activities. We can be big givers but not let the teaching affect our lives. We might call this "Christianity Lite".

The mismatch in expectation when a church leader is hired by a congregation can eventually cause severe problems. Without knowing it the people in the church transfer most of their hopes and dreams for spiritual and numerical growth onto the shoulders of the new leader. The church leader is delighted with the attention. In fact, what has happened is that the congregation now has the church leader on a pedestal. Then, as expectations are not met, the first voices of criticism are heard. *It's not my job, it's the church leader's*. We have a tendency in our generation to outsource certain aspects of Christianity, and mission is one of them.

## 5. I was never invited

Many people have come from generations of Christians who were born into the church. They had no choice in going, they just went. But those generations have come to a close. It is the end of blind obedience without the possibility of choice. We are now in a generation where people most certainly have a choice, a generation who want quality of life.

The truth is, there are many who are seeking, but they are not prepared to put up with Christianity stripped of its essential parts. It is a generation assailed with information and calls for attention from every communication platform – computers, mobile devices, advertising hoardings, and hundreds of television channels. It is a generation where even to mention Christianity is bordering on harassment and where those who don't keep their faith private are seen as fundamentalists. We now have an opportunity of entering a period of time when we can explore a Christianity that truly changes people.

If we were born into the church, we may never have really practised invitation. It is a foreign concept. Add to that the fear of being rejected, and it is an unwelcome one as well.

Finally, some of us think that those outside the church should make the first move – that they should be asking us about our faith or our church.

When it comes to inviting people to church, there's no doubt that making the first move is nerve-wracking, but where this issue is concerned I'm on the side of the person to be invited. While it can a scary business to invite someone, my research tells me that it is also nerve-wracking for the invitee to make the first move. They have to overcome the fear that they will be rejected by us, not to mention the more fundamental fear that they have not got their lives sufficiently in order to be acceptable to the church.

## 6. What if it damages my friendship?

Mark Twain once said:

> *I am an old man and have known a great many*
> *troubles, but most of them never happened.*[11]

One of the most powerful fears facing us, as we contemplate an invitation, is the fear of diminishing a relationship. I might lose a friend over this, or it might alter the relationship for the worst.

I think Mark Twain said it correctly – most of our perceived troubles never happen.

Recently someone told me they don't invite because they don't want to rock the boat. Many of us are for the quiet life. We live a life of tiptoeing around issues and challenges, never quite engaging. Of course it is possible that we might damage or even lose a friendship through inviting someone to take a closer look at Christ. More likely will be some change to the relationship. But then we have been asked to go and make disciples... and, who knows, we might even improve the friendship!

Nicodemus visited Jesus at night for fear of what his peers would do if they found out. He was not alone. In John 12:42 we learn that many in leadership believed, but because of the threat of the Pharisees they chose security over Jesus and decided not to go public with their faith at that time. A classic story of parents succumbing to peer pressure appears in John 9:18–22. Even after their son is healed of blindness they refuse to be grateful to Jesus, but put the blame on their son for the healing instead. Utter peer pressure!

It could never happen today...? How about this: "I might be seen as pushing my faith, or judging others." These are a couple of the countless fear-of-man examples that suffocate invitation, as we succumb to peer pressure.

Others say to me they can't invite their friend "because it might go wrong". They fear saying the wrong thing at the wrong time. But I say: one way to learn how to do something right is to do it wrong! Don't be afraid of getting it wrong – it may well lead to a new level of learning. Learn from your experience. God can take wrong and make it right.

## 7. Our services and people are unpredictable

This can be true, although I have noted that many churches are overcompensating by making their services predictable through rigorous planning. We have to be careful here, lest we forget we are not in the entertainment business.

There is a saying that perfectionism is the mother of procrastination. I was not surprised to hear someone say recently that they were not going to be doing any inviting until the church service was right! I regularly hear, "When we have more young people, then I will invite" or "When we have more activities, then I will invite" and so on. The church is never going to be perfect – or even perfectly predictable.

This is the number one reason church leaders give for why congregation members don't invite. And they don't necessarily help if they feed the expectation that this one hour per week is the be-all-and-end-all of the Christian life. Of course, as an act of worship it should be treated very seriously, but we should not lay so much store by having everything planned out to the last detail. Give God room to surprise you!

## 8. I fear the congregation will think my friend is not "our" type

One serial inviter told me recently that they were not afraid of hearing the word "no", they were more afraid of the response of the congregation to the person they brought along. This reason is unfortunately more common than we would like to think. It certainly gives us a great sermon title: "How can we invite when we fear what this congregation will think?" But, as we shall see later on, more than a sermon will be needed here if we are to create an invitational culture.

## 9. I am reticent

A reluctance to invite our friends to our present act of worship could conceivably be wisdom, but a reluctance to invite our friends to take a closer look at Christ and his church can never be right. Reticence can so easily masquerade as timidity. There are times in life when we must throw caution to the wind. We must lose our fear, or let our courage, strengthened by faith, attack our fear. In the Acts of the Apostles, Peter and John were cautioned by the authorities not to speak about the name of Jesus. They ignored the warning and threw caution to the wind by still speaking out. Timidity and over-caution are diseases that need to be treated with God's Spirit of power, love, and self-discipline. So if this is you, throw caution to the wind today and invite someone to take a closer look at Christ and his church.

## 10. Religion is a private matter

Invitation was always part of Christianity back in the beginning. Yet in our generation, Christianity appears to have become a private thing. When did faith become private? When you think about it, science is public, faith private; the arts are public, faith is private. Who says so? The same people who put us down with accusations of being pushy Bible-bashers.

And with friends the situation appears to be even worse. It is as though we are crossing a line, somehow abusing our friendship.

Very often I hear what seems like a reasonable point of view: we need in this day and age to take a softly, softly approach rather than a pushy approach. It sounds sensible... until we bring obedience into the picture. If God prompts us to invite someone and we translate that into a softly, softly approach, then are we not guilty of fearing man rather than God? We tiptoe around the issue. Was Jesus softly, softly or pushy, pushy? It seems to me that he was neither. He was just about his Father's business.

## 11. I don't want to be seen as strange

Noah looked strange building an ark in the desert. Sarah looked strange buying maternity clothes at ninety. The Israelites looked strange marching around Jericho blowing trumpets. David looked strange attacking Goliath with a slingshot. The Wise Men looked strange following yonder star. Peter looked strange stepping out of the boat in the middle of the lake in the middle of the night. And I love David's comment to his wife who was ashamed of his strangeness:

> I will become even more undignified than this, and I will be humiliated in my own eyes. (2 Samuel 6:22a)

We need to become less self-conscious and more like little children who love to explore the world around them. This is Eugene Peterson's definition of worship:

> *Worship is the strategy by which we interrupt our preoccupation with ourselves.*[12]

## 12. They might ask something about my faith

Or: "I am not going to invite someone for fear of cross-examination." In law, cross-examination is the interrogation of a witness called by one's opponent. It is the close questioning of a hostile witness. In the Great Commission, Jesus asks us to be his witnesses, telling people about him. Some of those opportunities will be easy and some will be hard or even hostile. But we will be following the example of our Saviour who was cross-examined by Herod and Pilate.

I meet people in my seminars who say that if they invite people to church, "They'll find out I am a Christian!" It's as though they wish to be in a witness protection programme. That is the protection of a witness whose life may be threatened if their identity or location is known by their (criminal) opponents. Some witnesses are provided with a new identity, and may live out the rest of their lives under protection. I have to say that there have been times in my life when I have hidden my identity in Christ, when I could have said something but didn't. I know first-hand how Simon Peter felt when he denied Jesus. But I have found the best witness protection programme ever:

> *fear not, for I am with you (Isaiah 41:10, ESV UK)*

## Dismantling the fear management system

These common reasons are our way of avoiding God's prompting in our lives. We have developed a sophisticated fear management system so that we don't need to mention the elephant in the room.

There are people out there God is asking us to invite, and we are avoiding his call. Meanwhile our fear hides behind distractions. We will do anything other than invite, even to the extent of reading books about it, hearing sermons about it, and yes, going to seminars like mine. We sit in home groups or cells where we study what we already agree on. We even blame people outside the church for not coming. We blame the media. This search for scapegoats shows that we have abdicated responsibility. We have not assessed honestly the true root of the problem. In psychology this is called avoidance behaviour. Basically we are avoiding our fear. In order to begin to tackle this paralysis we simply need to become consciously aware that fear is the only obstacle between us and mission.

And it is not just failure in invitation that church leaders and members avoid, but success. Not succeeding actually reduces the fear of failure. I remember one church leader going into panic when he heard that numbers were up at an event at his church. He was heard to say that "we will never be able to improve on that next year"! A one-time success instantly called in that church leader's mind for repeat-performance success – more ways to lose, more ways to fail. They are in limbo, opting for mediocrity and never embarking on new ventures.

I've said several times in this chapter that "there is truth" in many of the objections people raise. What truth and untruth can we find in each reason? As we look we find that each of the twelve reasons is in fact a distorted truth and leads to a more basic level of reasons. These include:

- We were taught not to speak to strangers.
- We were taught not to speak until you are spoken to.
- We were taught that we need to succeed.
- We should never appear as pushy.
- Why invite someone who has their life together?
- We worry about timing.

This more fundamental level is more concerned with what society and parent-figures have taught us. These things are deeply ingrained within our thinking and mission practice. Many people are not predisposed to talk – they don't talk on trains; they don't talk to strangers. Personally, I find such advice wrong-headed. What made sense as advice to a child should not carry over automatically to our adult life. There is no way for us to meet people and expand our circle of friends without being open to those we don't yet know (i.e. strangers). Any advice that advocates avoiding people guarantees that we start from a baseline of fear. When we have small circles of friends it is no wonder that we fear rejection from the few friends we have! Strangers can be friends just waiting to happen.

So we have distorted truth sold as received wisdom put on us by the church, where we now have to become passionate, or educated, or trained, or at least have some ability to tell our story with confidence. None of these things are wrong, of course, but when they are elevated as a necessity before we even go into mission, then they *are* wrong, and the cost of entry to become missional has become prohibitive.

## Naming the sin

This is why I have come to the conclusion that so many of us are following a toxic mission script. These false reasons should really be pinned up in our church, on display as our real creed – the one we really believe, because we have been misled. It is very important that we understand the reality of our situation, so that we can potentially change it.

> we take captive every thought to make it obedient to
> Christ. (2 Corinthians 10:5b)

How can we return to those places where wrong conclusions were formed, and help people unlearn and relearn at that level, so that their lives are governed by actuality and not illusion?

I think John Wesley can help us with the four questions that underpin his method:[13]

> What sins have you committed since last time we met?
> What temptations have you faced?
> How have you resolved those sins and temptations?
> What do you think might be sins and temptations that
> we can discuss now?

Wesley was on to something, but I think he was only revisiting early Christian practice. I think the early church was worried about its sins and we are not! I recall the Damascus Road experience when Luke recalls that Paul heard Jesus' voice asking why he was persecuting him. The fact that we could be persecuting Jesus through our sins is doubtless a novel thought to our generation of Christianity. We can so often think that the trouble facing Western Christianity lies outside the church, because people are not coming – failing to realize that the trouble could very well be on the inside. Whenever we refuse to keep growing at the prompting of God, our sins can grow instead.

Paul echoes this when he says

> *For I do not do the good I want to do, but the evil I do not want to do – this I keep on doing. (Romans 7:19)*

And the writer to the Hebrews:

> *let us throw off everything that hinders and the sin that so easily entangles. (Hebrews 12:1b)*

Jesus was constantly trying to expose the barriers to a full relationship with God. Sometimes he told a person to sell their possessions; sometimes they needed to leave home or change job. For it is not just the things we do that may be sin – it can equally be down to the things we should be doing but have shied away from. One of the Greek words for sin is *harmartia* and comes from archery: it refers to "falling short", when the arrow misses the mark.

Augustine challenges all of us not to look in the wrong places for the things which only God can provide:

> *Seek what you are seeking, but don't seek where you are seeking it.*[14]

But people are ever more reluctant to tell each other the truth about themselves, their weaknesses, their inadequacies. We even call it "abusive", damaging to people's self-esteem, to offer them realistic criticism, or set them tasks that will make them aware of how far they have to go. But in reality this indulgence and fear of hurting people's feelings is far more abusive in the long run. It makes it hard for people to gauge where they are, or to develop self-discipline. And such thinking certainly contrasts with the emphasis on repentance made by Jesus.

It was after John's arrest that Jesus came into Galilee, proclaiming the gospel of God, saying,

> *The time has come at last – the kingdom of God has*
> *arrived. You must change your hearts and minds and*
> *believe the good news. (Mark 1:15, J. B. Phillips)*

King David asked God to search his heart because he could not be sure of his own thinking (Psalm 139:23–24). He did not trust himself to be sufficiently objective when it came to assessing his own thoughts and motives, for sometimes the heart goes on autopilot and we don't really know why we do what we do.

One of the most comforting verses I have found to help us is the verse before the Great Commission. We all know the words of Jesus to his disciples before he ascended into heaven:

> *All authority in heaven and on earth has been given*
> *to me. Therefore go and make disciples of all nations,*
> *baptising them in the name of the Father and of the*
> *Son and of the Holy Spirit, and teaching them to obey*
> *everything I have commanded you. And surely I am*
> *with you always, to the very end of the age.*
> *(Matthew 28:18–20)*

But we can easily forget the context of this commission. Here is the preceding verse:

> *When they saw him, they worshipped him; but some*
> *doubted. (Matthew 28:17)*

Jesus sent eleven doubting disciples out on mission. Do you not find that interesting and comforting? It is interesting because it seems that part of the Great Commission was to deal with the doubts of the disciples; and it is comforting because my findings show that we have some of the same doubts, as expressed in the common reasons.

It did not matter that the eleven disciples had doubts. Even where they did not believe in Jesus, Jesus believed in them! That is what counts. If you are a follower of Jesus, Jesus believes in you.

When we share Christ's teaching with someone, the blessing can go both ways – the person receiving the teaching can be transformed, but so also can the person sharing. If you invite someone to take a closer look at the teaching, it may be just the right time for them. But it could also be the right time for the person sharing to grow in confidence.

It's a bit like a caterpillar crawling on the ground that one day thinks, "I was made for more than this." It makes the effort to crawl up a plant and weave a cocoon. And so, eventually, out comes a butterfly.

In sharing there may be effort in understanding the teaching, and then in overcoming the fear. But the result could be nothing short of metamorphosis.

# 3

## Facing the Fear

Confronting distorted truth or irrational perceptions may be good treatment for symptoms, but what about the cause?

Nestling below the distorted truth we find the fear of rejection. These fears sometimes surface in the reasons we give for not inviting, through words like "concern", "worried", "anxious", and "careful".

The belief that fear is harmful is universal, but God gave us fear to survive, not to paralyse us. God has designed the acute fear response as an adjuvant – protecting us through helping us to perform better. Think of David taking on a lion or a bear, only then to take on Goliath. David's time as a shepherd, including moments of acute fear, led to resilience and courage. If you've seen it before, and dealt with it before, you feel stronger.

Of course, not all fear is good. But, whereas the good kind may last only minutes or, at worst, hours, bad fear is chronic, dragging on for weeks or months or even years. Any original reason for the lingering sense of fear may be long gone.

So there are some positive outcomes of fear and rejection. We will discover that fear is one of the undiscovered discipleship tools for our generation, for from fear can come vision, resistance, and negotiation.

## Confronting the fear

The subtler forms of fear escape us – we have so many different words for them. Most of us, if challenged that we appear afraid, quickly say it is not true. And so we find it difficult to recognize fear in our lives. Here are some words we may employ that might give us a clue that we are working with fear:

*stressful*
*afraid*
*apprehensive*
*bothered*
*concerned*
*distraught*
*anxious*
*fearful*
*fretful*
*frightened*
*nervous*
*uneasy*
*diplomatic*
*worried*
*careful*
*sensitive*
*reluctant*

In the previous chapter, in looking at the twelve common objections to inviting, we found that fear was either explicitly stated or implied. This is not just an issue for our generation of Christianity attempting mission. Back in 1953 a survey was made of those attending training sessions for a Billy Graham crusade in Detroit. One of the questions was, "What is your greatest hindrance to witnessing?" Twenty-eight per cent felt it was the lack of real information to share. Twelve per cent said their own lives were not speaking as they should. Nine per cent said they were too busy to remember to do it. None said they didn't really care. But by far the largest group were the 51 per cent whose biggest problem was the fear of how the other person would react.[15]

So this is nothing new.

Here are some classic examples of fear in the Bible

- Adam and Eve were afraid of God after they disobeyed him.
- Abraham hid the identity of his wife for fear of what would happen to her.
- Moses was afraid as he did not know how to speak in public.
- The ten spies before the entry into Canaan feared the enemy.
- Saul feared the Philistines.
- Peter feared for his life in the courtyard after the arrest of Jesus.
- The disciples hid in the locked upper room for fear of the authorities.

If we ignore the emotion of fear, mission will be hindered. Fear drives us to avoid the thing we fear, and so we may never learn the truth – that it is not as threatening as we thought.

Even on the day of the resurrection, the followers of Jesus were afraid. Mary Magdalene, Mary the mother of James, and Salome visited the tomb of Jesus because they wanted to anoint the body of Jesus. They saw to their surprise that the stone at the tomb entrance had been rolled away. As they entered the tomb, they saw a young man dressed in a white robe sitting on the right side, and they were "alarmed". This is clearly another word for "scared to death"!

*"Don't be alarmed," he said. "You are looking for Jesus the Nazarene, who was crucified. He has risen! He is not here. See the place where they laid him. But go, tell*

48

> *his disciples and Peter, 'He is going ahead of you into*
> *Galilee. There you will see him, just as he told you.'*
> *(Mark 16:6–7)*

Their fear was understandable, but it resulted in an inability to speak. Happily for those of us who followed, they eventually overcame their fear and told the story. Which is why we can now play our part.

We should not ignore fear. In fact, we need to put faith precisely where our fear is.

The heart rate starts to pound, you know you are about to cross a line you may never have crossed before: you are just about to invite someone, or have a conversation about the Lord. Ever had that feeling? I think to some degree we have all had that feeling. I think Jesus anticipated this, and so he left us with these comforting words:

> *Surely I am with you always, to the very end of the age.*
> *(Matthew 28:20b)*

This is the essence of our faith and, surprisingly perhaps, we can only really test the depth of its meaning by taking our fear in our hands and starting to invite people to take a closer look at Christ and his church. As we do so we will find truly that the Father has not left us alone. Immanuel our God is with us.

Fear is anticipation of pain, but too often its bark is worse than its bite. Fear directs our attention to what we found frightening in the past. We don't take in the full meaning of what others are saying to us. Out thinking becomes immovable. We refuse possibilities unless they are really clear, and then we misjudge the risk.

In the Bible there are eighty clear cases of God saying, "Don't be afraid", and thirty close approximations. It is as if God were anticipating that fear was going to be a real area of difficulty for us, and so he reminds us again and again not to be afraid.

Susan Jeffers, author of the book *Feel the Fear and Do it Anyway*,[16] gives three general principles about fear that will help us:

- Fear never goes away as long as we continue to grow.
- We should get rid of fear by doing what we fear.
- All of us feel fear when we are on unfamiliar territory.

Point 1 might seem to contradict number 2, in that when you face a fear such as inviting someone and you go ahead and invite them, the fear does go away. However, when God asks you to invite someone else, some of that fear may well return and the battle have to be refought. This is how we grow in becoming responsive to God's missional prompting.

As we deal with fear, we can ease away a tangle of obstacles. God says, "I am with you, therefore there is no need to be afraid." This is one of the most undervalued good news statements of Scripture.

Listen to how the presence of God plays out with Jacob:

> *I am with you and will watch over you wherever you go, and I will bring you back to this land. I will not leave you until I have done what I have promised you. (Genesis 28:15)*

These are God's words to Jacob and to us.

There are many other instances of this. The boy David brings some food for the brothers who are at war facing the Philistines. David goes to the battlefront and immediately says to the brothers, and I paraphrase: "Who is that idiot there?"

Of course, David is talking about Goliath, a giant of fear who has paralysed the army of Saul. As the story plays out we see that fear is conquered by faith in God. The army of Saul is awoken from its apathy by a boy with five stones and a sling... but more importantly, by a boy with faith who knew that God was with him.

There will be times when you want to give up: remember God is there. There will be times when you will deny Christ: remember God is there. There will be times when you are in the sweet spot of life: make sure you remember that God is there too!

## Apathy – who cares?

Church leaders sometimes ask me why their congregations can appear so apathetic to mission. I believe apathy is a masking agent. In the field of chemistry, a masking agent is used in chemical analysis to react with substances that may interfere in the analysis. Infamously, in the world of sport, such a masking agent is used to hinder the detection of banned substances or illegal drugs such as anabolic steroids or stimulants. In a parallel way, we can regard apathy as a masking agent for fear, making it difficult to detect.

As I travel the world, I find Western Christianity in general suffering from a malaise made up of boredom, apathy, and general depression. I am often asked how we should deal with the apathy in the pews. I reply that people seem to be at their best when they are striving to fulfil good and worthy ideas, especially when they are swept up by a great idea. Wherever you find boredom, you will find the absence of a great idea. When we are gripped by a single, strong idea, our self-worth is increased and we find purpose.

Henry David Thoreau said:

*We have only to move confidently in the direction of our dreams, to meet with a success unexpected in uncommon ideas.*[17]

Joy and contentment come when we strive for our goals, not just when we reach them. Beneath the surface of our lives there are deep reservoirs of ability. The direction required to combat the malaise comes from God, but it can often be identified through our fears, hesitations, anxieties, and worries. We must constantly choose growth over safety.

Many people are doing just enough to get by – they like safety. We can be creatures of inertia, for most of us don't like change. We wait until something works and then we copy it. We don't want hassle. We can be addicted to mediocrity without realizing it. We all have aspects of safe living about us.

What aspect of you died a long time ago, that just didn't get buried yet? Apathy is like being sedated; it creates a lethargy. Apathetic people rarely turn up in my seminars, for obvious reasons, but on occasions I do meet them. Their reasons for not inviting differ from the common ones:

- Even if they do come, how do you know people will stay?
- We have had our fingers burnt in the past.
- We are short of time and this is way down the to-do list.

In my thinking about apathy, I have come to the conclusion that apathy is a form of arrested development. The apathetic person is locked in a childhood approach to life, with little control over their environment. They hope and expect someone else will do it for them.

In this way, apathy is a coping strategy to bolster a sense of self-worth. Most people fail in the Christian life not because they aim too high and miss, but because they aim too low and hit.

Indifference remains a major, if disregarded, aspect of the moral life. The confession "We have not loved our neighbours as ourselves" becomes a moral question. What are the things we have left undone? What are we missing?

We are snoozing. Just because we walk and talk, that does not mean we are truly awake. Zechariah was not physically asleep when an angel roused him "as a man who is awakened from sleep" (Zechariah 4:1, NASB).

Jesus compared the church to virgins who "all got drowsy and began to sleep" (Matthew 25:5, NASB).

From the beginning, the voice of Satan has had this lulling effect on humankind. Eve's excuse for disobedience was, "The serpent hath caused me to forget" (Genesis 3:13, YLT).

And so Paul writes:

> *Awake, sleeper, And arise from the dead, And Christ will shine on you. (Ephesians 5:14, NASB)*

But there is hope. Apathy is something we tend to acquire (often for peer acceptance), which means it can be unacquired. But it will take effort. The longer a habit has been around, and the deeper it has been engraved, the more energy it will take to change. Getting something going always takes more energy than keeping it moving.

## No fear

I remember a television documentary where an operator in an emergency call centre described their work. When the call comes in, the operator said there must be no fear at their end of the line. There is nothing tense in their voice – in fact they "take the caller's fear" as they lend the person at the other end of the phone their faith that the situation will be handled well. This I believe is what happened with the boy David – he "took the fear" of Saul's army and replaced it with his own faith that God was with them.

In the story of the burning bush, we find Moses in fear questioning the sanity of God who is asking him to go back to Egypt. In the end God says to Moses, "I will certainly be with you" (Exodus 3:12, HCSB). Now, when God tells us not to be afraid, he shows that he has already anticipated times when we will be – and he wants to reassure us.

Fear distorts the truth and triggers poor judgments which can lead to serious consequences. When Abram goes to Egypt (Genesis 12:10–20) he says to Sarai in verse 12:

*When the Egyptians see you, they will say, "This is his wife." Then they will kill me but will let you live.*

So he makes out that she is his sister, but this leads to all sorts of complications with the pharaoh, who finds out the truth in the end.

But Sarai too allows her fear to cloud her judgment. Years later, when she fears that God will not give them the son he had promised, she says to her husband:

*"The Lord has kept me from having children. Go, sleep with my slave; perhaps I can build a family through her." (Genesis 16:2)*

As Moses leads the people out of Egypt and through the wilderness, God provides quail, and strange food called manna:

*"Each one is to gather as much as he needs …"[said Moses] "No-one is to keep any of it until morning." (Exodus 16:16, 19, NIV 1984)*

But out of the fear that the food would not be provided any more, some of them kept part of it back for the next morning – and it was full of maggots and began to smell.

Then, as they leave the wilderness and enter the Promised Land, the new leader, Joshua, is told to be strong and courageous. It does not take too much imagination to realize that this was because he was afraid.

And then try to discern Simon Peter's distorted truth, his interior creed or mission statement, as he lets both himself and his Lord down. This is what he had already said to Jesus, in a spirit of bravado:

> *"Even if all fall away on account of you, I never will."*
> *"I tell you the truth," Jesus answered, "this very night, before the cock crows, you will disown me three times."*
> *But Peter declared, "Even if I have to die with you, I will never disown you." And all the other disciples said the same. (Matthew 26:33–35)*

But can you sense the fear in Peter as he denies Jesus for the first time?

> *Now Peter was sitting out in the courtyard, and a servant-girl came to him. "You also were with Jesus of Galilee," she said. But he denied it before them all. "I don't know what you're talking about," he said.*

And can you sense the fear building as the accusation is widened and Peter denies Jesus for a second time?

> *Then he went out to the gateway, where another servant-girl saw him and said to the people there, "This fellow was with Jesus of Nazareth." He denied it again, with an oath: "I don't know the man!"*

And can you see how easily fear leads us to rejecting the one we love, as Peter denies Jesus for the third time?

> *After a little while, those standing there went up to Peter and said, "Surely you are one of them; your accent gives you away." Then he began to call down curses, and he swore to them, "I don't know the man!" Immediately a cock crowed. Then Peter remembered the word Jesus had spoken: "Before the cock crows, you will disown me three times." And he went outside and wept bitterly. (Matthew 26:69–75)*

You reap what you sow, or as we may put it today: actions have consequences. Fear without faith in God leads to captivity, whereas fear faced with God leads to an awareness of his presence.

Two ancient words in the Old Testament point us to the two sides of the fear-faith ledger – *behold* and *beware*. "Behold" these examples of faith, but "beware" these examples of fear. Distorted truth leads to the same captivity we see in our Bible stories, and the twelve common reasons are causing the results we are currently finding in Western Christianity.

> *Fear of man will prove to be a snare, but whoever trusts in the Lord is kept safe. (Proverbs 29:25)*

Many of these "beware" examples are of people who feared man rather than God. Aaron yielded to popular clamour and made the calf. Saul cared more to be honoured among the people than to please the Lord. Pilate feared that a charge would reach Caesar, and so he violated his conscience. At the root of insecurity – the anxiety over how others think of us – is pride. This pride is an over-the-top desire for others to see us as important and admirable. Insecurity is the fear that they won't, that instead they will see us as deficient. We are caught in the snare that is the fear of man over the fear of the Lord.

I believe that we need to put truth where there is untruth, and there we will find the power of the gospel. But it is the *experience* of the truth that will set us free (John 8:32). The word for knowing the truth in the Greek is *ginosko*. This refers not to an accumulation of information so much as to the experiential practice of the truth – knowing in the doing. John says we should do the truth. We are the most educated Christians in history but we don't *ginosko*!

Jesus' three years of public ministry are one long intervention of helping people to see the truth, even as he came up against untruth. We find this brutal honesty in his encounters with the Pharisees.

> *Now then, you Pharisees clean the outside of the cup …*
> *(see Luke 11:37–39)*

> *Woe to you, teachers of the law and Pharisees, you*
> *hypocrites! You travel over land and sea to win a single*
> *convert, and when you have succeeded, you make them*
> *twice as much a child of hell as you are.*
> *(Matthew 23:15)*

In the Sermon on the Mount, Jesus tells us how to combat fear (Matthew 6–7). He says we are to *take no thought for tomorrow* as we resist the temptation not to *lay up for ourselves treasures on earth*. Reminding us that even *the lilies of the field are clothed in splendour*, he enjoins us to *ask and it will be given*. To do the truth – to do what God says, is to build *a house on rock* and not on shifting *sand*.

Jesus is pointing out one way after another of dealing with fear:

- Don't worry about the future.
- You can lay up treasure in heaven.
- God is generous – the items you need will come (maybe not what you want).
- Your prayers will be answered (maybe not in the way you expect).
- When trouble comes, what matters to you will stand firm.

## Reading our fears

You may have observed the vivid imagination of young children when they jump in the air and believe they have just flown. This can stay with us as adults. Sometimes (for the most creative minds) it turns us into writers, painters, lyricists, entrepreneurs. But for others, our vivid imagination becomes disordered fear. Fears allow us to project ourselves forward in time. But in order to regain our vivid, innocent imagination we need a change of strategy.

Karen Thompson Walker speaking at TED[18] on "What Fear Can Teach Us", said:

> We need some steps. Step 1, let's call fears stories, with characters, with us being the main character. In our fear-stories there are plots with beginnings, middles, and ends. Our fear-stories have suspense – what will happen next? In Step 2, instead of acting as the author of our fears, how about if we act as the reader of our fears?

We can then decide as the reader what aspect of the fear is worth listening to. The reader needs the cool judgment of knowing that Immanuel our God is with us. I believe God is often the author of our vivid imagination, but we tend to respond to the worst possible outcome in the plot (perhaps it is the easiest to imagine). For the Christian, Step 3 is to find God in the middle of our fear-story. Fears allow us to look at what the future might be while there is still time to influence how the future might play out.

## Turning fear to our advantage

Fear can have hidden benefits. I was talking with a retired US Navy pilot with a second career as a church leader. A fighter pilot is taught about the importance of fear. As you take off from the aircraft carrier, adrenaline is rushing, your hearing becomes acute, and your mind is able to process data quickly. Fear makes you hyper-aware and is a natural survival method.

Antonio Damasio is a professor in the area of neuroscience and neurobiology at the University of Southern California. At a talk at a TED Conference[19] he said that "the emotions have a way of modelling what you are going to do next". We can "use emotions for future planning". So it is as though the emotion of fear is a sophisticated guidance system. I am not saying this is true in every situation, but we do well to look out for God's call in our fear.

God called Gideon out of the barn, and he called the disciples out of a locked room. God called Moses out of forty years of exile, and he called Esther from the comfort of being the queen. All these examples have fear at the beginning of the call – fear that provides a level of guidance within it.

So today God calls and draws us from one place to another. We were made to know God. Far from being our enemy, our fear can lead us to a vision of the future. But when we give in to fear and develop anxiety, this is simply to repeat failure in advance.

When the twelve spies went to spy out Canaan (see Numbers 13–14), all of them saw the same things – a land flowing with milk and honey – but they didn't all come to the same conclusion. Fear led ten to say that the people in the land were giants and God's people were grasshoppers compared to them; whereas two spies saw the same thing, and even acknowledged that there were going to be difficulties and strong opposition, but concluded that there would be no problem taking the land because God was with them.

How could there have been two different opinions? Fear is a matter of perception which affects point of view: some people feel flying is scary; some people don't. Some people feel spiders are scary; some people don't. Fear is not knowing: it is an uncomfortable feeling. But for others it is an opportunity. For some, invitation is a scary activity, while for others it isn't. I think the ten spies developed a dose of anxiety, and that foretells a future that is not going to happen. It is dangerous paralysis, an exaggeration of the worst possible "what if". But even more importantly anxiety uses the same energy as faith. The Indo-Germanic root *angh*, from which we get our words "anger" and "anxiety", "angst" and "angina", means to constrict. It is a constriction of the natural impulses. Jesus in the parable of the talents seems to suggest that whatever you don't use you lose. Apply that to faith, and we have to admit that unused, it declines.

Most of our lives we spend our time resisting fear; just as Franklin D. Roosevelt famously said, we have a fear of fear, such that what we really call fear is not necessarily the direct experience of fear, so much as the feeling of resisting fear. We are just trying to keep it at arm's length. The goal should be to let ourselves feel afraid when we feel afraid, and to actually experience the fear. To say, "Fear is happening – but that's OK," and not to fight it off.

There are two key Hebrew words for fear which will help us to look more into the way that fear can lead us to a vision of the future.

*Pachad* is a fear of projected or imaginary fear – those worst-case scenarios, as when you are asking someone on a date. This is more aligned to chronic fear. This type of fear is self-fulfilling. A self-fulfilling prophecy is a prediction that directly or indirectly causes itself to become true, by the very terms of the prophecy itself. This fear predicts the future but does nothing to alter it. The ten spies had this type of fear. There they were, heading to the Promised Land, but in the end they didn't get there. Their future got cancelled. They sold out their future to get current relief, but sadly by not taking a risk they lost their destiny.

*Yirah* is a fear that comes upon us in a space that is larger than we are used to, or in the presence of something sacred or divine. It is when you touch an authentic dream, a vivid "*kairos* moment" when time is revealed in surprising depth and clarity. This is more aligned to acute fear. Interestingly, *yirah* not only means "to fear", it also means "to see". Twelve spies all saw the same thing: ten looked and saw and compared themselves with the enemy; two saw things in relation to God.

A similar thing happened to Elisha and his servant (see 2 Kings 6). The servant came in panicking to Elisha, saying they were surrounded by a vast army. But Elisha had the eyes of faith and prayed that the servant might see what he saw – that they were in fact surrounded by horses and chariots of fire. To see or not to see – that is the question! *Yirah* is the type of fear that is mentioned forty-four times in the Old Testament. This sense of the presence of God has been lost in the concept of fear in our modern thinking.

Acute *yirah* fear is an aesthetic experience: our senses are operating at their peak, and we are truly present in the current moment, trembling with excitement at the thing we are experiencing. It is when we are fully alive and just know that we were made for this moment.

I strongly suspect that the vast majority of us have shut off our senses and deadened ourselves to what is happening the majority of the time. In fact we have been anaesthetized.

Through a stimulus (which we often sense as fear) God brings us from unconsciousness to ever deeper consciousness, and awakens our conscience to hear the call of God.

Of course, in any fear there can be a mixture of *pachad* and *yirah*. But if you can identify *yirah* in what you are feeling, you can actually sense the sacredness of the event, and welcome it, and live in a more peaceful way.

Think about a roller coaster ride. Part of what moves people to get on board is the fear – except they don't call it fear, do they? They call it excitement. What makes it possible to embrace a fearful situation and see it as exciting and exhilarating? In the case of a roller coaster, you see others doing it and having fun. No one flew out of their seat, and all the cars stayed on the track. So your mind becomes convinced that you won't die. I suspect that the popularity of gambling through the lottery and licensed bookmakers is merely another version of the roller coaster. It is an attempt to experience the excitement of fear.

But *yirah* signals the sacredness of what you are touching. It is a thin space between us and God where we can sense the call of God beckoning us onwards. Although this fear is thin, it feels thick – overwhelming and daunting.

## Coping with no

*If the home is deserving, let your peace rest on it; if it is not, let your peace return to you. (Matthew 10:13)*

These are the instructions given by Jesus when he sent the twelve disciples out on mission. What my research across Western Christianity shows is that many of us have never got over the last person saying no to us. We have been disturbed by the experience. In other words, our peace did not return to us; fear has taken its place.

Earlier we said that success is in the act of invitation itself, not the response. Our analysis of fear maintains this emphasis on the inviter, while of course not forgetting the person invited.

We do not often know just what stage our invitee has reached in their journey towards faith – nor who else is going to play a role. In this way our missional lives can be likened to a jigsaw puzzle. Our puzzles arrive incomplete, and we never know when another person might provide a missing piece. Conversely, we never know when we are carrying the piece that might help others complete their puzzles.

When the prophet Samuel was trying to solve a puzzle, God gave him the following advice:

*But the Lord said to Samuel, "Do not consider his appearance or his height, for I have rejected him. The Lord does not look at the things people look at. People look at the outward appearance, but the Lord looks at the heart." (1 Samuel 16:7)*

Don't pray for inviting to be easier – pray you will be better; don't pray for fewer problems – pray for more expertise. Don't ask for it to change out there – ask God to change you. God is doing something in us, not just through us.

Northrop Frye, in a book of lectures called *The Educated Imagination*,[20] speaks of three uses of language. The first has to do with the simple awareness of the facts of life. It contains nouns and adjectives, it concerns itself with what *is*. The second language is concerned with what one must *do* to get along in the world. In its most developed form, it is the language of science and technology, the language of our work where peer pressure makes conformity the norm.

The third language is concerned with what *might* or *could be* – we might call this the language of hope. It can be God's language, as he speaks in a voice too quiet for panic to hear. But with practice we can begin to discern God's still, quiet voice. (What has that quiet voice been saying to you?)

As we go deeper in our relationship with God, we can be well aware of our fear, but now it becomes a compass, not a barrier. It becomes a way to know what to do next.

In the Acts of the Apostles, there is a story about Paul and Barnabas in Antioch speaking to the crowds. As they spoke, they were confronted by a group of Jews.

> When the Jews saw the crowds, they were filled with jealousy. They began to contradict what Paul was saying and heaped abuse on him. Then Paul and Barnabas answered them boldly: "We had to speak the word of God to you first. Since you reject it and do not consider yourselves worthy of eternal life, we now turn to the Gentiles." (Acts 13:45–46)

It can't have been easy, being rejected by your own people, and having to take abuse. But they used the fear in a dangerous situation as a compass to point them in the direction of the Gentiles. In this way they did not give up inviting, they just turned to a new set of people.

We have swapped the fear of the Lord for the fear of man. We need to maximize the fear of the Lord and minimize the fear of man. It is *yirah* versus *pahad*!

And perhaps we are expending too much energy on the question, "What should we fear?" when actually we should be asking "*Whom* should we fear?" And the "whom" is the Lord. This is the fundamental difference between *pahad* and *yirah*, between fear of the unpredictable, life's ups and downs – and fear of a God who loves us.

Know before whom you stand.[21]

The incredible thing is that in fearing God, in having true *yirah*, we begin to release ourselves from *pahad*, the many destructive fears that affect us.

## Let your fear mark a new beginning

Fear, in fact, is very helpful for our survival, but more than that, Proverbs says:

*The fear of the Lord is the beginning of wisdom (Proverbs 9:10)*

*The fear of the Lord leads to life; then one rests content, untouched by trouble. (Proverbs 19:23)*

Now, if it is true that the fear of the Lord is the beginning, the starting point of all that is vital, then we should be seeking it, because it produces wisdom, life, and contentment. Urgent research needs to go into this area. Perhaps theologians and scientists might come together in the field of psycho-neuroimmunology (the study of the interplay between the brain, the mind, and the body's defences). While we expect that chemicals have a physical effect on the brain, the idea that distorted thinking replaced with truthful thinking has the same effect seems really surprising. Nonetheless, it is clear that it does.

The spiritual song inspired from the valley of the dry bones featured in the book of Ezekiel reminds us of the connectedness within our bodies – "the knee bone connected to the thigh bone" and so on. Ezekiel found himself surrounded by the bones of the dead – and God commanded him to preach to them! And to pray over them. When he obeyed the command, Ezekiel saw those dead bodies brought back to life.

Like Ezekiel we are surrounded by people who show no signs of life – be that within the church, without the signs of life in all its abundance; or outside, where spiritual death seems to dominate our world. And, like Ezekiel, we have been invited to tell the dead that they can live.

The fear of man was a problem for the early church as well. Here is Paul:

> *The Spirit you received does not make you slaves, so that you live in fear again (Romans 8:15a)*

You can take people out of slavery, but you can't take slavery out of the people quite so easily. Ask Moses. He had to deal with the whingeing and complaining of the children of Israel, who before long decided they would prefer a return to slavery in Egypt over freedom in the wilderness (forgetting that it was a step towards the Promised Land).

Moses did not begin well. His fear gave rise to both resistance and negotiation in his dealings with God. When he is first called, Moses resists no less than five times.

First he says, "Who am I to do this?" He clearly doesn't believe in himself.

Second, "When I come to the children of Israel, they are going to ask me in whose name I am acting."

Third, "Even if I believe in myself, they won't believe in me."

Fourth, "I am no good at public speaking."

And fifth, "Send someone else. In fact, why not send my brother?"

In other words... "Here am I... send him!" (Exodus 3:11 – 4:17)

I call this "the burning bush syndrome". Most of these negotiations between us and God go on in the privacy of our own minds, never really seen by others, but they are all too real.

Eventually Moses learned to stop trying to negotiate with God. His fear subsided as he sensed that God accepted him and wanted to communicate with him. He had given Moses freedom to be a friend!

The really great news about this burning bush syndrome is that God is looking for people who have no confidence in themselves. We see this in the story of Gideon too. The angel of the Lord is dispatched to Gideon, and in a fantastic piece of exaggeration says:

*O mighty man of valour. (Judges 6:12, ESV)*

Can I beg to differ? Here we find Gideon threshing wheat, hidden in the barn for fear of the Midianites. But at least Gideon joins in the heavenly comedy by saying, "Have you got the wrong address?"

*Because I am the least of the least.*

God responds that he is looking for someone like Gideon, who doesn't think that they can do it, so that his glory can be seen.

There is a fabulous story in the book of Acts where God directs in mission through an instruction and a bit of negotiation which then propels amazing growth.

> *Now there was a disciple at Damascus named Ananias.*
> *The Lord said to him in a vision, "Ananias."*
> *(Acts 9:10a, ESV)*

I am so glad God is on first-name terms with his servants, and wants to have an ongoing relationship with us.

> *And he said, "Here I am, Lord." (verse 10b, ESV)*

Here we have echoes of the boy Samuel's attentive response to God's call.

> *And the Lord said to him, "Rise and go to the street*
> *called Straight, and at the house of Judas look for a*
> *man of Tarsus named Saul, for behold, he is praying,*
> *and he has seen in a vision a man named Ananias come*
> *in and lay his hands on him so that he might regain his*
> *sight." (verses 11–12, ESV)*

This is a very precise instruction. But then we get the fear turning up in the story, and a piece of negotiation is about to take place.

> *But Ananias answered, "Lord, I have heard from many*
> *about this man, how much evil he has done to your*
> *saints at Jerusalem. And here he has authority from the*
> *chief priests to bind all who call on your name. (verses*
> *13–14, ESV)*

Don't you just love it when we find a saint telling God something God already knows? Fear causes us to freeze, fight, or flee. But there is some negotiation space for Ananias with God, for God answers the question.

*Go, for he is a chosen instrument of mine to carry my name before the Gentiles and kings and the children of Israel. For I will show him how much he must suffer for the sake of my name." (verses 15–16, ESV)*

And Ananias goes.

When you see a fork in the road, take the one that points towards God. Jonah infamously decided to run in the opposite direction and ended up in the belly of a sea creature for a three-day mini-break. Now, actions do not emerge from nothing – they faithfully reveal what is in the heart. Jonah's dash in the opposite direction to the one God commanded brought his true feelings to the surface: Jonah did not want Nineveh to repent! Might this sadly be true of some members in your own congregation?

And what are you afraid of? What are the fears that are holding you back from living life to the full, the way God intended?

And, thinking of Jonah, what are your fears about what God might be doing in your life and in the life of your church and in the neighbourhood? This is where we need to identify our fear.

C. H. Spurgeon said:

*The very gift of faith is a hint to you that you will need it – that at certain points and places you will especially require it – and that at all points and in every place you will really need it.*[22]

But the most marvellous news is that we don't need to be afraid, for *God is with us*.

Consider these words of God to Moses (Exodus 3:12):

*Certainly I will be with you (NASB)*

God would not let him go alone!

Every imperative in Scripture is built on an indicative; to put that another way, every command is built on a promise. The command is "Don't be afraid" while the promise is "I will be with you". So to get the promise we have to do the command.

Consider these words from Moses to Joshua:

> *The Lord himself goes before you and will be with you; he will never leave you nor forsake you. Do not be afraid; do not be discouraged. (Deuteronomy 31:8)*

It is a long journey from fear to the knowledge in our whole being that God is indeed with us. It is easy to say or sing "the Lord is my shepherd", but much more rare to know that the Lord is *my* shepherd. It is written on tons more gravestones than on the lives of people.

It is easier to sing "Immanuel – our God is with us" than to be experiencing it on a daily basis. But this is the journey of faith. Some Christians look to the future with apprehension, while others look to the future with anticipation. Why is there such a difference? Jesus said, "Go [into the future] and make disciples." I believe that those who look to the future with apprehension don't have the future well designed. They make hesitant, uncertain steps – if any steps at all. But listen to the promise of Jesus: "lo, I am with you always" (Matthew 28:20, KJV). The person who looks to the future with anticipation is the one who sees clearly the promise of Christ to be with them every step of the way.

Our God is all-knowing and all-powerful and all-present. Therefore I can trust that whatever my fears might be, they are tiny in comparison.

Look at Joshua's final words to Israel. They bear his testimony, the story of his experience of passing from fear to faith, into the presence and acceptance of God:

*One man of you shall chase a thousand, for*
*the Lord your God is He who fights for you, as He*
*promised you. (Joshua 23:10, KJV)*

Read these beautiful words of Scripture and be comforted:

*When you pass through the waters,*
*I will be with you;*
*and when you pass through the rivers,*
*they will not sweep over you.*
*When you walk through the fire,*
*you will not be burned;*
*the flames will not set you ablaze. (Isaiah 43:2)*

Vaccination is the administration of antigenic material to stimulate the immune system to develop adaptive immunity to a pathogen. In the light of the passages we have just read, all Christians need to report for a daily vaccine. When taken, it strengthens the spiritual immune system that is our faith.

Easy to say, but less easy to know when you are going through a difficult and traumatic situation. But that is precisely when we need faith – faith alongside our doubts! Would God rescue Daniel from the lions' den? Would God rescue Shadrach, Meshach, and Abednego from the fiery furnace? It was not certain, but faith was strong.

What makes a farmer plough the ground and plant in the spring, if the farmer couldn't see the vision for the harvest? Is it possible to see the finished harvest? Yes, with the eyes of faith. Faith is the ability to "see" things that don't yet appear to our sight.

# 4

# Responding to Rejection

Perhaps the most devastating finding in my research is the less public phrases people use to express how they deal with rejection – when people say no.

- I felt inadequate.
- It made me feel ignorant.
- It was an attack on my ego.
- It shook me to the core.
- I felt undermined.
- It belittled me – made me feel small.
- It diminished me.
- I feel exposed.
- It has sapped my confidence.
- It has dashed my hopes.

Seeing these phrases is like turning over a societal rock, with all manner of horrible things living beneath it. These phrases reveal untold painful stories – untold because they are concealed by great professional success: I have had lawyers, doctors, teachers, and business people all use similar language.

We are often encouraged to quit whining and get over our wounds, but I believe acknowledging the feeling can lead to healing.

Developmental psychologist Dr Gordon Neufeld in his talk[23] on "Making Sense of Anxiety" said this:

> The mind tunes out the perceptions that would lead to vulnerable feelings. We actually can't see that which would make us feel too bad, that which alarms us. On the peripheral we can see the common reasons, but because we can't see the ones at the centre it accentuates the common reasons. The mind orphans the feelings of alarm, divorcing them from the real cause. The mind is a meaning-making organism – it's got to know what is wrong, so it simply starts to invent what is wrong (which is where we get distorted truth).

Professor James Pennebaker, chair of psychology at the University of Texas, [24] highlights the small words *I, you, me, we, us,* pointing out their tremendous ability to illuminate who we are and how we are feeling. Pennebaker studied the nature of traumatic experience and its links to physical health. He found that people were much less likely to get sick if they talked to other people, and that keeping a secret is somehow toxic. That's a high price for secrecy.

If we are going to deal with rejection, I think we need to help people tell their stories. They need to share the secrets behind the fears with someone they deem socially important – and come out knowing that they are still a socially acceptable human being. Confession and absolution have health benefits!

Francis Bacon, in *The New Organon,* published in 1620, wrote:

> Memory is assisted by anything that makes an impression on a powerful passion, inspiring fear, for example, or wonder, shame, or joy.[25]

Someone once said that there is nothing wrong with a no unless you are on the receiving end! It is amazing how one experience can plant seeds to grow a fear.

Of course, getting a no is not the answer we want, while a yes affirms us. The no makes us feel that we have somehow failed. Perhaps we said or did something wrong. Perhaps an uncomfortable truth about us has come to light – were we too pushy, for example? We have been brought up in a society that is intolerant of failure, and any perceived mistake can lead to humiliation. We are obsessed with perfection and hiding problems away. We have not really been taught what to do with failure. It is like a dead end. If we get a no, we are thinking, "What do I do now?" We assume there is no more room for discussion. This leaves a gap in the relationship that may need to be repaired, as we are eager to recover the previous relationship. This is why, for many of us, invitation is a no-go zone. When you have emotionally invested in a relationship, what seems like the rejection of your Christian faith can feel like a game changer for that friendship. And so many of us never bring the subject up again. Meanwhile the hurt remains. Being turned down can feel like a slight on our whole being.

So how else would we help congregation members who fear rejection? Maybe we need to remind ourselves… Who do we know in the Bible who was rejected? Begins with a "J"…

This is a matter of discipleship:

> Remember what I told you: "A servant is not greater than his master." If they persecuted me, they will persecute you also. If they obeyed my teaching, they will obey yours also. (John 15:20)

If we are ever going to do anything for Christ, then sooner or later we will be rejected. Plain and simple!

If you have not been rejected lately, you have to wonder whether you are in the game.

This is not a problem just for our generation. Back in the late nineteenth century, G. K. Chesterton said:

> *Christianity has not been tried and found wanting; it has been found difficult and therefore not tried.*[26]

Richard Rohr, in his book *Breathing under Water*,[27] says:

> *Christianity has become theory over practice.*

Here are two more verses which make the point:

> *Consider it pure joy, my brothers and sisters, whenever you face trials of many kinds, because you know that the testing of your faith produces perseverance. Let perseverance finish its work so that you may be mature and complete, not lacking anything. (James 1:2–4)*

> *Not only so, but we also glory in our sufferings, because we know that suffering produces perseverance; perseverance, character; and character, hope. And hope does not put us to shame, because God's love has been poured out into our hearts through the Holy Spirit, who has been given to us. (Romans 5:3–5)*

So… are you in the game?

Now, it is true that the enthusiasm of new converts can do much to wake us up to the power of invitation. But for how long? I have seen new Christians happily inviting their friends… until they work out that invitation is not what we do around here! Then they discover a double rejection effect: not only might their non-church friends turn them down, but it seems their new church friends may present a problem too – sending them a message (directly or indirectly): "We don't do that type of thing around here."

Who loves me? Who doesn't love me? Have I done something wrong? Have I been let down? The central concern of human life is attachment – just listen to our pop songs. We just don't spend enough time teaching about attachment and reminding our people that we will all be rejected at some point and that is part of the deal. Even when we feel rejected God is still calling us.

## Are you up to it?

The Bible is full of illustrations of God calling and prodding people into service in spite of their overwhelming sense of inadequacy. Some were thrust into ministry environments almost against their wills. And Jesus was constantly stretching the disciples' faith. In the story of the feeding of the 5,000, Jesus said to the disciples:

> They do not need to go away. You give them something to eat. (Matthew 14:16)

It was a test of their faith. Like us, the disciples made excuses and told him things he already knew:

> "We have here only five loaves of bread and two fish" …
> [Jesus said,] "Bring them here to me".
> (Matthew 14:17–18)

In other words, just bring what you have and I'll work with that. When we do that we will experience Immanuel God with us.

God has an incredible way of proving the faith of a disciple. It is as if stress can trigger faith, given the right conditions.

We see this in nature. Take fire, for example. The jack pine tree has cones which are serotinous. When there is intense heat, normally over 50°C (122°F), the cones open and release seed. This happens during a forest fire. So rather than seeds being released when they are mature, the concept of serotiny means they are released in a very difficult environmental situation.

As in nature, so in spiritual development. The fires of stress and opposition can stimulate our faith in the God who is with us. Indeed, in the famous case of Shadrach, Meshach, and Abednego, their faith was literally tested by fire. They not only survived – they were promoted.

The apostle Peter declared:

> These have come so that the proven genuineness of
> your faith – of greater worth than gold, which perishes
> even though refined by fire – may result in praise, glory
> and honour when Jesus Christ is revealed. (1 Peter 1:7)

No wonder disciples have to be in training. This can work in a number of ways, such as with self-denial, but – as with Shadrach, Meshach, and Abednego – God sometimes confines us, and narrows our focus as well. God did this when he let Joseph spend years in prison, and Moses in exile, and David on the run from Saul, and even with Jesus in the wilderness. It is a maturation means that God uses. Talent and gifting seem to grow by their very confinement.

So have you been tested lately?

> Again Jesus said, "Peace be with you! As the Father has
> sent me, I am sending you." (John 20:21)

Here is the message in plain language: you are going to get nailed. But you can have peace. As both the apostle Paul and James say in

77

those verses, there are some incredible benefits from facing our fears and our trials, even in the face of rejection. We can't learn anything if we are not prepared to fail or at least be vulnerable to the possibility of failing. Vulnerability is a voluntary transfer of power and control. And God did it first. He sent his Son into the world, and he sent his Spirit at Pentecost. Mission is God giving himself up, laying aside his divine prerogatives and taking our humanity. God became vulnerable as a baby – and remained vulnerable right up to the cross.

God seems to use the vulnerable and despised – like David, the nobody that nobody knew; like Rahab, who went from call girl to called girl; and like Gideon, the least of the least.

Jesus continues the practice when he sits down with a lonely Samaritan woman (see John 4). In today's world you might think that this was not a good use of his time if the gospel was going into Samaria. We would not be sending a woman with a "reputation" as the first missionary to the town.

Jesus trained his disciples to live vocationally: he used a sea storm which they could in no way control to embrace a life of prayer in which they might participate in God's control. When Paul was shipwrecked, he prayed. He prayed through the darkest part of the night and received the gospel message, "Do not be afraid."

For development and maturation you need vulnerability. When the emotion of fear is not faced, you stop developing and remain immature. The primary prerequisite for learning is curiosity. To be curious means that you care about something – and if you care, then you can be hurt.

We need to build on solid ground. How does God see us? When we are building our identity on how others see us, we are building on sand.

## Tending your wounds

If you have ever felt any of the following wounds, then the good news is that God may be seeking you.

- inadequate
- ignorant
- an attack on ego
- shaken to the core
- undermined
- diminished
- belittled
- exposed
- confidence sapped
- hopes dashed

This last one – disappointment – is particularly relevant when considering rejection by a family member or close friend, because these can wound us deeply. People say they don't invite because they fear the outcome.

These are the wounds of congregation members coming to the surface as we consider going into mission. The wound of rejection distorts our view of mission. And the wounds seem too well aimed and far too consistent to be accidental. I believe that they are aimed in the area of who we are meant to be.

Each one of us has the presence of the past in our lives – things that are still affecting us. Just because a page is torn off the calendar does not mean that that unit of time has ceased to exist. If you don't transcend your wounds, you transmit them. They then develop into various diseases – indifference, indecision, doubt, worry, overcaution, pessimism, and complaining.

Now, these diseases could be viewed as the problem, but I believe they are actually the solution to a deeper problem which we see emerging from within the wounds. They are basically there to buffer an underlying need not to be emotionally vulnerable. They provide a sense of self-protection.

These well-aimed wounds then begin to distort our thinking and focus our reactions at keys points in our life. In psychology this is something called "weapon focus", which affects the reliability of eyewitness testimony. Weapon focus occurs when a witness to a crime diverts all their attention to the weapon the perpetrator is holding, thus missing other details in the scene, which in turn leads to memory impairments later on.

The weapon being pointed at each Christian in mission is the prospect of rejection, and it is distorting our vision and affecting our memory. We forget things because of the wounds. Consider these biblical injunctions to keep our memories keen:

> then take care lest you forget the Lord, who brought you out of the land of Egypt, out of the house of slavery. (Deuteronomy 6:12, ESV)

> But the Helper, the Holy Spirit, whom the Father will send in my name, he will teach you all things and bring to your remembrance all that I said to you. (John 14:26, ESV)

Biblical scholar Walter Brueggemann once said that one of the most important things in being a Christian is "to practise memory in a world of amnesia".[28]

We have this incredible "forgetory".

Rejection is mentioned very early on in the story of Adam and Eve and appears to have started off a chain reaction. The rejection of God by Eve, when she believed the lies of the serpent, leads to Adam following suit, and this then leads to self-rejection:

*Then the eyes of both of them were opened, and they knew that they were naked; and they sewed fig leaves together and made themselves coverings. (Genesis 3:7, NKJV)*

This was followed by the fear of rejection:

*And they heard the sound of the Lord God walking in the garden in the cool of the day, and Adam and his wife hid themselves from the presence of the Lord God among the trees of the garden. (Genesis 3:8, NKJV)*

This leads on to the rejection of others:

*Then the man said, "The woman whom You gave to be with me, she gave me of the tree, and I ate." And the Lord God said to the woman, "What is this you have done?" The woman said, "The serpent deceived me, and I ate." (Genesis 3:12–13, NKJV)*

*Rejection of God*

*Self-rejection*

*Fear of rejection*

*Rejection of others*

The echo of the Garden of Eden reverberates right down to our generation. Separation alarms us and makes us fearful.

But the great news is that these wounds can be brought to the surface, and through mission, God is working in us and through us to bring healing.

*I am the Lord who heals you. (Exodus 15:26)*

Fears thrive in silence, in the darkness. But bring them into the light and the healing process can begin.

In a wonderful maternal image, God as seamstress sews leather garments for Adam and Eve (Genesis 3:21). So the first thing God does after creation itself is to cover the shame of his new creatures. This suggests to me something fundamental within any authentic experience of God. He will seek to cover our shame.

We might be through with our past, but our past is not through with us. Once Jesus had raised Lazarus from the dead, there was still a job to be done:

*"Unwrap him…" (John 11, see verse 44, NLT)*

This is the God who wants to

*[heal] the broken-hearted and [bind] up their wounds. (Psalm 147:3)*

There is a correlation between the depth of someone's wound and the distance we have to travel with them in order to get them to open up and reveal their pain. Or another way of putting it: wounds are like a multi-storey building; the higher it goes, the deeper its foundations must go, and you have to drill down deeply to find the foundation of the wound.

We generally work hard to keep our wounds hidden. This is

82

to protect ourselves. You only open a wound in order to let a doctor or nurse tend to it. Sometimes churches do not feel like places of healing.

We often say, "How are you doing?" in church circles – it is a form of greeting. But we are not really asking how someone is really doing; people sense this, and so they keep their wounds hidden. As a result, some accidentally transmit the wounds, while others manage them.

God takes a very strange course with us where healing is concerned, often taking us back to the very place where we have been wounded. One of my major wounds is from being rejected in childhood. It seems cruel to say that God placed me in the hands of church leaders who for ten years would reject my communication to them on a daily basis. But bizarrely I have grown through the experience and have learned so much from the rejection. God is dealing with my overdependence on others by sending me on mission trips away from my family. It is bittersweet, but I have learned in my times of seclusion to be more dependent on God.

A similar story of growth was experienced by many of our biblical figures. Queen Esther moved from beauty queen – concerned with creating a certain impression on the king and others – to "if I perish, I perish" (Esther 4:16d). She learned to face her fear and the possibility of rejection, even death, and through it she herself became who she was meant to be. Esther lived in a literal "comfort zone", confined and walled in, in the king's harem, unable to leave without his permission. We are not always so different. Motivational speaker Jim Rohn said this:

> The same walls we build to keep out disappointment
> also keep out happiness.[29]

The pursuit of happiness is one of the most familiar concepts for human thriving. But joy (which is better than happiness) is the gigantic secret of Christianity. Joy is not a requirement of Christian discipleship; it is a consequence. Rohn is basically saying that if we don't face our fear of being disappointed, we also lose some of the positive benefits of being a Christian.

The Gospel of Luke (10:1) tells us that Jesus sent out seventy-two of his disciples and told them to go and tell people that the kingdom of God had come near. He prepared them for the mission by telling them that they would meet people of peace – already prepared for the message – and people who would reject them and the message. For those who accepted, Jesus' instruction was to stay with them. But in the case of rejection, Jesus said, move on! When the seventy-two returned, Luke says they came back "rejoicing". They faced their fears of rejection, they got rejected, but they found joy.

## Dealing with disappointment

Fear has friends: discontent, dissatisfaction, regret, and boredom. Henry David Thoreau wrote:

> *Most men lead lives of quiet desperation and go to the grave with the song still in them.*[30]

"Sleeping Beauty" is a familiar childhood story, but like many fairy tales it is an allegory for all of us, as we fight our way through life. Like Sleeping Beauty, we need to wake up and become all that we are meant to be.

This sleep or drowsiness is expressed by Christian and non-Christian alike in many different ways. One is through security. We can be more concerned about our pensions than we are about living. We are deferring our God-given dreams until some later point – as though we were saying, "I am not changing the world but I have got retirement benefits."

Bronnie Ware is an Australian nurse who spent several years working in palliative care with patients in the last twelve weeks of their lives. She recorded their dying revelations in a blog called "Inspiration and Chai", which gathered so much attention that she put her overall conclusions into a book called *The Top Five Regrets of the Dying*.[31]

All the regrets had elements of fear about them, but the number one regret of the dying was this:

*1. I wish I had had the courage to live a life true to myself, not the life others expected of me.*

It is easy to see how many dreams have gone and are going unfulfilled, because we are more concerned about what others think than what God has us designed to be.

*2. I wish I hadn't worked so hard.*

Ware says, "All of the men I nursed deeply regretted spending so much of their lives on the treadmill of a work existence."

I think there might be many reasons for continuing to work without joy, but perhaps the greatest reason is the fear of losing God's provision if we leave our secure jobs.

*3. I wish I'd had the courage to express my feelings.*

Ware observed, "Many people suppressed their feelings in order to keep peace with others. As a result, they settled for a mediocre existence and never became who they were truly capable of becoming. Many developed illnesses relating to the bitterness and resentment they carried as a result."

We fear saying what we really think, and as Ware found this can often lead to disease, or at least a life of mediocrity.

*4. I wish I had stayed in touch with my friends.*

We often don't have the time to deepen our friendships because we fear the loss of time in doing so. "Time for what?" we should ask ourselves. Does it really matter so much?

*5. I wish that I had let myself be happier.*

Ware comments, "Fear of change had them pretending to others, and to their selves, that they were content, when deep within they longed to laugh properly and have silliness in their life again."

## Where is my security?

At some point, our preoccupation with being safe will get in the way of living full lives.

Thoreau wrote:

> *Oh God, to reach the point of death only to realize you have never lived!*[32]

This desire to be secure becomes disordered when fear gets in. Our security should come from being at the centre of God's plan for our life. When God takes us through trials and tribulations, the fear of God is our security, and the gift of the Holy Spirit can help us resist evil and pursue good.

Faith's friends: "love, joy, peace, forbearance, kindness, goodness, faithfulness, gentleness, self-control" (Galatians 5:22–23a).

Not many of us like dramatic, uncomfortable, personal change, yet it is possible to face discomfort. Look at Paul's words to the church at Philippi:

*I have learned to be content whatever the*
*circumstances. I know what it is to be in need, and I*
*know what it is to have plenty. I have learned the secret*
*of being content in any and every situation, whether*
*well fed or hungry, whether living in plenty or in want.*
*I can do all this through him who gives me strength.*
*(Philippians 4:11–13)*

*Cradles of Eminence*[33] by Victor and Mildred Goertzel is a book which produced a fascinating study involving 413 "famous and exceptionally gifted people who have helped change the world". The authors spent years attempting to understand what produced such greatness; to find a common thread that ran through all of these outstanding lives. Surprisingly, the most outstanding fact was that 392 – nearly all of them – had to overcome the personal fears associated with great suffering or failure in order to become who they were.

Brené Brown, research professor, University of Houston, says:

*Vulnerability is our most accurate measurement of*
*courage.*[34]

This is because, when it comes to fear, we not only want to know the future, we want to control it as well. It is a person of great moral courage who steps vulnerably into the future not knowing the outcome in advance. For those of us who choose the illusion of control of the future over vulnerability, we should know that those powers are reserved only to God. I suspect our problem here is that we don't just want to be like God, we want to be God. G. K. Chesterton said:

*Courage is almost a contradiction in terms. It means a*
*strong desire to live, taking the form of a readiness to*
*die. He that shall lose his life, the same shall save it.*[35]

Caleb was one of the two spies who felt that the children of Israel should enter the land of Canaan, but was outvoted by ten other spies. Caleb had to wait forty years to fulfil his dream. I love Caleb's courage as he went for his dream of winning the high mountain. Look at his words:

> It may be that the Lord will be with me, and I shall be
> able to drive them out … (Joshua 14:12, NKJV)

Do you see the uncertain outcome Caleb was willing to risk because he trusted completely in God's word?

Nehemiah put faith before fear. Being sad before the king was punishable by death, and so when the king sees that Nehemiah looks sad he is understandably afraid and yet declares the truth.

> I was very much afraid, but said to the king, "May
> the king live for ever! Why should my face not look
> sad when the city where my ancestors are buried lies
> in ruins, and its gates have been destroyed by fire?"
> (Nehemiah 2:2–3)

Bev Shepherd, in her book *Insight into Stress*,[36] says:

> Courage comes from knowing that our ultimate destiny
> is in God's hands.

We can learn two things about fear from Caleb and Nehemiah. They contradict the following statements.

- Since I feel fear, my dream must not be from God.
- I can't go forward unless God takes away my fear.

As we have seen, fear is in fact often intrinsic to the call of God.

Moving from the illusion of control to vulnerability is a long walk, from "What will people think?" to "Know that Immanuel our God is with us". It is much easier to believe in God than to trust in God. Belief can be cerebral, but trust has to involve vulnerability on our part.

When someone says that they don't invite because when a person says no, it might bring their own faith into question, they are missing an important truth. We see the questioning of our faith as a bad thing, whereas surely to have our faith tested has advantages. It can strengthen that faith. James writes:

> *you know that the testing of your faith produces perseverance. (James 1:3)*

I think God is saying he is glad when we are weak and vulnerable, for

> *Not by might, nor by power, but by my Spirit, says the Lord… (Zechariah 4:6, ESV)*

Therefore it doesn't really matter what God has given us to do; if he is helping us, then we can do it. There is no saying what a man or a woman can't do when God is with them. Give God to them, and they can do all things. When we run in the opposite direction from uncertainty and vulnerability, we run from the abundant life. Uncertainty is beautiful and certainty, were it to be real, would be moral death. Uncertainty means the future is open to creativity and possibility. Jesus calls us to life abundantly, not life redundantly.

We human beings are distinct from the rest of nature. The acorn becomes an oak by means of automatic growth. The kitten becomes a cat without any effort on its part. Nature and being are identical in creatures like these. But human beings only become what God meant them to be by a long line of decisions made daily as we face our fears and follow the call of God.

Expecting rejection can be a reflex action – an involuntary reaction to a stimulus. This is often how we will make a decision – we've not even consciously thought about it. Each of us is automatically defensive. I think this is because, unconsciously, we sense that we are precious. I am reminded of the commandment that we are to

> *"Love your neighbour as you love yourself." (Mark 12:31a)*

If we combine this involuntary reaction to rejection with our fear, the fear can actually identify something worth saving. This then helps us marshal all our capacities.

So if fear and rejection are causing the church to stumble, how do we address the problem?

# 5

## Addressing the Problem

The greatest way to change another person's behaviour is to change their paradigm – to alter the map of how they see themselves. This will then change how they see their role and responsibility.

### What do we think we know?

There is a sad story of Jacob being shown his son Joseph's coat of many colours by his other sons. Jacob sees that the coat is torn to shreds, with blood on it. Jacob then declares:

> *"… Joseph has surely been torn to pieces."*
> *(Genesis 37:33)*

Remember, there were no DNA tests available to him. This was all the evidence he was going to have – this, and the false testimony of Joseph's brothers. And so Jacob believed this piece of distorted truth for more than ten years. He lived with a paradigm that said his son was no longer alive.

Now, Joseph may have been dead to Jacob, as he was no longer with him or his family, but over a decade later the same sons came to Jacob and told him that Joseph was alive. The Bible records his reaction like this:

*The spirit of … Jacob revived. (Genesis 45:27)*

This whole episode in Jacob's story reminds me that while there are things that we know, there are things that we know we don't know, and things we don't know we don't know. But there are also things that we think we know but we don't know!

Now, when we become aware and we start believing the truth, there is the possibility of personal revival and the healing of wounds. There is a saying, "Deal with the lie and the fear will die." We feel the cobweb of fear but don't deal with the spider of the lie. Go for the cause, not for the consequence.

The book of Numbers has an instructive scene in which the Israelites in the wilderness are overtaken by a craving. They are perfectly well fed on manna, yet they are protesting for the meat, fish, melons, cucumbers, garlic, leeks, and onions that they say they got "for free" in Egypt. They also say they have starving stomachs and "nothing at all, but this manna to stare at" (see Numbers 11:6). The suggestion? Things were better before they left Egypt.

Moses and God are incredulous. What's up with these people? We might agree – until we ask, "Does this happen to me?"

Firstly, why are they lying? Their memory of Egypt is distorted. The people did not have lots of free delicacies – they were enslaved. They didn't even have enough straw to make bricks. In addition, their situation doesn't seem to call for negativity. The manna isn't just to stare at, they eat it aplenty, with a double portion on Fridays!

The truth is, they had a distorted view. They needed to have their mental blueprint changed. Albert Einstein said:

> *We can't solve problems by using the same kind of thinking we used when we created them.*[37]

But the apostle Paul said:

> *Do not conform any longer to the pattern of this world,*
> *but be transformed by the renewing of your mind.*
> *(Romans 12:2, NIV 1984)*

It is difficult to have your mind renewed and transformed if you do not know what you are thinking in the first place. This is why the first tool I give in my seminars is to ask the question, "Why are we not going to be doing any inviting?" This establishes the thinking of the church. We can then recognize our present thinking and replace it with what God's thinking.

Brendon Burchard is a bestselling author in the area of motivation. He came up with an acronym RWID to encourage people to look at their thinking. It stands for the "Relative Weight Importance and Duration"[38] of a thought. How much credence or weight am I giving to the thought, how long will I let it draw my attention? Duration is everything. The longer a distorted thought stays on my mind, the more real it becomes, and then the more trouble I am in.

I mentioned earlier that I felt the twelve common reasons for not inviting are the creed of the church, because I can go anywhere in Western Christianity and find the same reasons. A creed is a statement of shared beliefs. And, sadly, it is the ongoing conversation between God's people and God. Can you imagine how God must feel as God hears us repeat this creed over and over again?

- I suffer, and I don't want my friend to suffer.
- My friend won't want to go as they said no to me last year.
- We have no non-churchgoing friends.
- It's the church leader's job.
- I was never invited – I was born into the church.

- What if it damages my friendship?
- Our services and people are unpredictable.
- I fear the congregation will think my friend is not "our" type of person.
- I am reticent.
- Religion is a private matter.
- I don't want to be seen as strange.
- They might ask something about my faith, and I wouldn't know what to say.

Where is God in any of the reasons? We can sing "Immanuel our God is with us", but when asked a simple question, what are the reasons we are not going to invite our friends? All twelve answers come without a sense of God's presence with us.

## Inviting God

In this book we are spending most of our time with two aspects of inviting: inviting our friends to take a closer look at Christ; and being invited by God to partner in his mission. But there is a third aspect that must not be overlooked: we must intentionally invite the presence of God into our acts of worship.

It is clear to me that we are, as a whole, not sensing the presence of God in our worship. God, of course, is with us, but inviting the presence of God might help congregation members to start to recognize the presence of God.

*Come near to God and he will come near to you.*
*(James 4:8)*

94

## The fear of fear

In addition to believing the truth and inviting the presence of God, we can deploy other emotional, mental, and physical strategies. Let's look at what others have said about dealing with shame, fear, and rejection.

William Shakespeare wrote this in *The Tragedy of Julius Caesar*:[39]

*Cowards die many times before their deaths;*
*The valiant never taste of death but once.*
*Of all the wonders that I yet have heard,*
*it seems to me most strange that men should fear;*
*Seeing that death, a necessary end, will come when it*
*will come.*

Shakespeare saw that cowards die a thousand deaths because of their shame, which eats at the soul in a thousand different ways. It creates a gulf between your mind, your heart, and your soul, between how you believe people perceive you as a person and how they really do. You become lower than death – a thousand times lower. The valiant rush in to join the battle. They may taste death, but it will never be more than once. They will never feel shame. In fact they will be held by others in great admiration. Death will only come once in their lifetime.

In his oath of office, President Franklin D. Roosevelt said:

*Let me assert my firm belief that the only thing we have to fear is ... fear itself – nameless, unreasoning, unjustified terror, which paralyzes needed efforts to convert retreat into advance.*[40]

We all remember the part where he says, "The only thing we have to fear is fear itself", but the other parts we usually miss: fear is unjustified and stops us from advancing.

That said, Roosevelt left out the best part – the reason we do not need to fear. Here is the version I much prefer:

*Do not be afraid ...*

And what is the reason?

*... for I am with you ... (Jeremiah 1:8)*

*... for the Lord your God will be with you wherever you go. (Joshua 1:9)*

We have managed not only to ignore Roosevelt's famous phrase and God's promise, but we have designed fear of failure into our whole way of life. We have decided that it is best to avoid risks and to stay safe.

A philosopher of today called Will Smith – also known as the Fresh Prince of Bel Air – recently said (in a YouTube video of *Inspirational Words of Wisdom*):[41]

*I'm motivated by fear of fear. I hate being scared to do something. I think what developed in my early days was the attitude that I started attacking things that I was scared of.*

Which restated goes like this:

*Do not be afraid ... for I am with you. (Jeremiah 1:8)*

Will Smith has also missed out the best bit!

*... for I am with you.*

God is speaking through these opinion-formers, even though they do not reference God's part in all this, or his offer to be with us. If we as Christians don't tell the good news to the world – that we don't have to be afraid, for God is with us – then a form of the news without God will be told by the opinion-formers of the world. But "Don't be afraid, for God is with us" is the true antidote that the world needs – for fear, anxiety, worry, and stress. Maybe we should try out the antidote and then pass it on to our neighbours, relatives, and friends!

Seth Godin recently said:

> *Instead of fighting … anxiety, dance with it. Welcome it. Relish it.*
>
> *It's a sign you're on to something … When we welcome a feeling like this, when we embrace it and actually look forward to it, the feeling doesn't get louder and more debilitating. It softens, softens to the point where we can work with it.*[42]

In his new book, *Uncertainty*, Jonathan Fields says we need

> *training in the alchemy of fear, turning fear from a paralytic force to abundance.*[43]

We need to be anxiety- and fear-aware. This means that fear is acknowledged as a reality but not embraced as a lifestyle. That lifestyle of fear is referred to as "stress". We can add value to people by pointing them to Christ who said, "Fear not." People suffer from life paralysis. We miss so many opportunities for fear of ridicule or rejection.

There is something really significant about the fact that the most repeated command in Scripture is, "Do not fear." There is nothing God cannot take care of for us.

In the film *The Life of Pi*, the main character is shipwrecked with a tiger and fears that he will either drown or be eaten by the tiger. During the course of events, he utters these profound words about fear:

> *I must say a word about fear. It is life's only true opponent. Only fear can defeat life. It is a clever, treacherous adversary. It has no decency, respects no law or convention, shows no mercy. It goes for your weakest spot, which it finds with unerring ease. It begins in your mind always. One moment you are feeling calm, self-possessed, and happy. Then fear, disguised as mild-mannered doubt, slips into your mind like a spy. Fear which is just an impression triumphs over you.*[44]

Health psychologist Kelly McGonigal, in a recent TED talk entitled "How to Make Stress Your Friend", apologized for making stress (extreme fear) the enemy. She has changed her mind about stress. McGonigal says that recent research confirms that

> *people who experienced stress but did not view stress as harmful were healthier.*[45]

If you change how you think about stress, you can change your body's response to it. Your pounding heart is preparing you for action, and your faster breathing is taking oxygen to the brain. This is an indication that your body is rising to the challenge. Thus your body is telling you that it is preparing to face the challenge. So any strategy that keeps you from facing your fear is a mistake in the long run. If you avoid a fear for too long, it will own you. Ask someone in the medical profession: they deal with the consequences of fear in so many medical fields.

To overcome the fear of failure is to have something worth failing for. There is nothing really wrong with fear. As we said earlier, we have simply exchanged the fear of the Lord for the fear of other people, and it is a terrible deal for us.

So what is worth failing for in your Christian life? After God gave his own Son for us, isn't it worth being rejected on behalf of God?

First Responders receive a place of honour in our generation. These are the brave men and women who respond to emergencies. Even as the rest of us perhaps run away from an emergency situation, these people are moving towards the danger. First Responders face fire, danger, death, and so naturally they regularly have to overcome *fear* just to do their jobs.

We admire such bravery because we aspire to it ourselves. So I wonder… could we use the concept of First Responders to tackle our own fear as it arises? Instead of running away from fear, or avoiding it, as the fear arises within us, let's start moving towards it.

## Embracing the fear – in love

Another approach can be found in the first letter of John:

> *There is no fear in love. But perfect love drives out fear, because fear has to do with punishment. The one who fears is not made perfect in love. (1 John 4:8)*

So if perfect love casts out fear, then we could look at fear and love as opposite points on a continuum.

**Fear–Love Continuum
In Invitation**

Fear ←——————————→ Love

Self-protecting                                          Self-giving
Move away from others                   Move towards others
The more fear the less                    The more love the less
love                                           fear

Fear is self-protecting, in that it moves us away from others. And the more fear we have, the less love we have. Whereas love is self-giving.

This continuum is played out in our Bible stories. We see it in the Garden of Eden with Adam and Eve in total anxiety that God will discover their actions. We see it in Moses as he hears the voice from the burning bush telling him to go to Egypt. His fear-based protestations move him away from his people, not towards them.

This type of fear appears to be a consequence of not doing what God has asked us to do. There is no fear, however, if we set ourselves to trust him:

> When I am afraid, I put my trust in you.
>   In God, whose word I praise—
> in God I trust and am not afraid.
>   What can mere mortals do to me?
>
> All day long they twist my words;
>   all their schemes are for my ruin. (Psalm 56:3–5)

Later, Moses can have an ongoing conversation with God as he leads the children of Israel. Abraham appears to have overcome his fear as he offers Isaac. Fear subsides as these men of faith sensed that God accepts them and wants friendship.

*In the fear of the Lord there is strong confidence ...*
*(Proverbs 14:26a, NASB)*

## The "No Quotient"

This has been a particularly good approach for me. What is your "No Quotient"? How many noes are you prepared to take for Christ? When I first started to pursue a movement of invitation, I had soaring expectation followed by crushing disappointment. I immediately faced a lot of negative comments, among some positive.

So I decided to steel myself to make ten communications a day to church leaders, requesting a conversation about invitation. I did this for ten years – ten communications a day by email, phone, or letter. Each day I received nine noes for every ten requests. Some days I just wanted to give up. But I have found that I need to make the ten communications in order to find the one church leader who is ready for the conversation.

I don't blame church leaders, for many of us are very busy, doing important work. But I want to let you know what it takes. So in order to write this book I have had to face a lot of negative interactions. But there is a plus side: most of the thinking in this book has emerged from the negative interactions.

When I have plucked up the courage to ask why someone says no – always a good question to ask, by the way – I have received whispers, nudges, and prompts from God. And there are many biblical stories that correspond with these rejections, some of which became part of God's purposes: so Leah was the wife Jacob rejected, but from her God produced Judah, and from Judah came David, and then later Jesus.

The life of Abraham was full of disappointment, disillusionment, and contradictions.

*I am going to send you out.*

*Where?*

*I will tell you later.*

*I will give you a land.*

*Where?*

*I will tell you later.*

*I am going to give you a child.*

*How?*

*I will tell you later.*

*Sacrifice your child to me.*

*Why?*

*I will tell you later.*[46]

Nevertheless, despite disappointment, disillusionment, and contradictions, Abraham was described in the hall of faith (Hebrews 11).

We find in Egypt that despite the whole nation of Israel being rejected and put into slavery, there was a multiplication factor happening. I think there is a law God has placed in the universe that says: unless there is a mini-death, like a grain of wheat falling into the ground and dying, there won't be any fruit.

*But the more they were oppressed, the more they multiplied and spread ... (Exodus 1:12)*

102

*Mini-deaths*

*"Unless a grain of wheat ..." (see John 12:24)*

*Suffering and death*

*Resurrection and transformation*

To do effective outreach, the Christian must die to themselves; it just comes with the territory. The heart of the matter is the heart of the believer. But we have little tolerance for disappointment nowadays – we seem more taken up with a sense of entitlement.

The only sense of entitlement that the boy David had was the sense that God would be with him. Recall those incidents that God brought David's way: David now uses them to speak to Saul about taking on Goliath.

> *The Lord who rescued me from the paw of the lion and the paw of the bear will rescue me from the hand of this Philistine. (1 Samuel 17:37)*

The paw of the lion and the bear! And we are afraid of the word "no"! David argued from past deliverances that he should receive help in a new danger. He had developed grit and was prepared for a struggle. Jesus continued this "discipleship by incident" by taking the disciples out in a boat and into a storm – for lessons to be learned and for the possibility of transformation. As Jacob learned, God sometimes wants to wrestle with us.

I love Eugene Petersen's *The Message* translation in Paul's letter to the church at Ephesus:

> *No prolonged infancies among us, please. We'll not*
> *tolerate babes in the woods, small children who are an*
> *easy mark for impostors. God wants us to grow up ...*
> *(Ephesians 4:14)*

God does not want us to remain as we are. God leads us towards growth. I was brought up on the stories of Shadrach, Meshach, and Abednego, and I still remember the title of the Sunday school lesson: "Think it not strange that you face the fiery furnaces of this world".

It is counterintuitive, but it seems struggle and pain open up space in the heart for joy. I love the old saying:

> *Life is like an onion: you have to peel it one layer at a*
> *time, and sometimes you cry.*

At times these are tears of joy.

Wouldn't it be interesting to find the NQ of your congregation? What if you could gather together ten congregation members? Then you all covenant together to invite one person each. Once those invitations have been made, you come back together again and count the yeses and the noes. Now, if it is as testing as my ratio, and you end up with nine noes to one yes, then at least you will know how many noes you have to go through to find that "person of peace" (see Luke 10:6). And when you do get to a yes, there will be joy; while the noes build resilience.

We should take lessons from our children. What does the word "no" mean to a child? Almost nothing.

*I can tell you the current solution to the missional problem very easily: we are not hearing enough noes.* More noes lead to yeses. I am only writing this book because I have heard more noes than the average Christian. But there is no disgrace in hearing noes. After all, God has faced more noes than we can imagine.

> And the Lord told him: "Listen to all that the people are saying to you; it is not you they have rejected, but they have rejected me as their king. (1 Samuel 8:7)

The more practice in hearing noes we have, the better we will get at finding yeses. In this type of exposure therapy, practice strengthens you. Practice does not make perfect, but practice does make improvement. We learn to experience *no* so often that it loses its power over us. As we become practised in facing our fears, we become more of the person God meant us to be.

## It takes courage

Rollo May, in his book *The Courage to Create*, writes:

> Courage … is the foundation that underlies and gives reality to all other virtues and personal values. Without courage our love pales into mere dependency. Without courage our fidelity becomes conformism.[47]

Courage comes from the French word *coeur* which means heart. Our heart pumps blood to arms, legs, arms, brain, and all the vital organs. In the same way, courage makes possible the Christian virtues as embodied in the fruit of the Spirit.

> But the fruit of the Spirit is love, joy, peace, forbearance, kindness, goodness, faithfulness, gentleness and self-control. (Galatians 5:22–23a)

Courage produces patience. In mission for God, sometimes you just have to be patient. But nowadays we want patience without delay! I love the old-fashioned word for patience – long-suffering. Today we don't even want short-suffering. Compare long-suffering with today's call for immediate results: if we can't have instant satisfaction, we give up. We need to combat this thinking in mission and become patiently impatient, holding the desire for a result in tension with the need to wait.

"No pain, no gain" is an exercise motto that promises greater rewards for the price of hard, patient, painful work. So competitive professionals such as athletes and artists endure pain and pressure to achieve professional excellence. It is not so different for the invitational disciple. To become a serial inviter there will be pain; but it will be worth it.

> *No discipline seems pleasant at the time, but painful. Later on, however, it produces a harvest of righteousness and peace for those who have been trained by it. (Hebrews 12:11)*

In the discipline of mission, as we use our invitational muscle, we have to face the pain of rejection; but if we do it often enough, right living will result, as we face our fears and come to a place of peace.

## Forgiving those who say no

Courage helps us to develop forgiveness, for we need to bear with people who reject our invitations. Many of us have never got over the last time someone rejected us. It takes courage to forgive. Offence, rejection, and ridicule can all help us to cultivate a spirit of forgiveness.

## *Keeping on keeping on*

Courage helps us to develop persistence, but we want persistence without obstacles! Someone once said:

*If you can find a path with no obstacles, it probably doesn't lead anywhere.*

Invitation is a Christian practice that allows us to explore uncertainty, risk, and exposure to criticism. In the early church the disciples were exposed to all three of these. As they moved from place to place, driven by persecution, they faced uncertainty: was God going to be with them? They faced risk – Paul narrowly escaped with his life. They were exposed to criticism from the authorities, both religious and civic. And yet the good news made progress. When it comes to faith, and being in mission, circumstances cut both ways. A positive event can adversely affect faith or strengthen it. Adverse circumstances can damage an individual's faith or deepen it. Listen to the apostle Paul:

*I have worked much harder, been in prison more frequently, been flogged more severely, and been exposed to death again and again. Five times I received from the Jews the forty lashes minus one. Three times I was beaten with rods, once I was pelted with stones, three times I was shipwrecked, I spent a night and a day in the open sea, I have been constantly on the move. I have been in danger from rivers, in danger from bandits, in danger from my fellow Jews, in danger from Gentiles; in danger in the city, in danger in the country, in danger at sea; and in danger from false believers. I have laboured and toiled and have often gone without sleep; I have known hunger and thirst and have often*

*gone without food; I have been cold and naked.*
*(2 Corinthians 11:23–27)*

And all we need to be concerned about is getting a rejection! You can't know who you are simply from standing on the mountaintop of success; you learn more in the valley of rejection.

Compared to the early church, we in the Western church are pretty much free from serious danger. What we fear nowadays is not really menacing. We might test a friendship over an invitation, but we are not going to risk our home or our life.

Yet we continue to shun risk, even if it often amounts to little more than the possibility of embarrassment. We do it automatically. That is why we must make a deliberate search for the fear in our lives, and take a risk after facing the fear.

If you squeeze a tube of toothpaste with the top off, what is inside comes out. In the same way, once you go into mission, or mention the possibility of inviting someone to take a closer look at Jesus Christ, what is inside the heart comes out. This is one of the by-products of invitation as a mission approach. I refer you back to the reasons that we don't invite: all the immaturity stored in our inner lives starts to come out. (By the way, so does the mature thinking.) In this way, invitational mission becomes part of a maturing process.

## The invitation clock

This is a way of looking at what is happening to the person we are inviting. It helps us to recalibrate success and re-establish faithfulness.

Imagine a clock face and think of both hands pointing at twelve. At twelve o'clock, whatever you say to people, they will say yes to your invitation. You might have said, "You won't want to come to my church, it's a bit rubbish, and I don't know why I go, but do you want to come?" And they will say yes, because they are at twelve o'clock in their relationship with God. God has already got there before you. They are just 100 per cent ready for an invitation.

At three o'clock on the clock face, whatever you say to the person you meet, they will completely reject you, and God, and probably say something like, "You must be joking… *me* go to church? Are you mad?" But now you know that they are at three o'clock in their present relationship with God.

At six o'clock when you invite them, they will say to you, "I have thought about this… but you are all hypocrites." They have a very high standard for their Christianity, and they are currently thinking about it. You have probably struck a nerve by allowing them to take the lid off their internal conversation with God. But at least now you know they are at six o'clock in their relationship with God.

When you invite the person at nine o'clock on the clock face, they will ask you something concrete, like, "When does the service start?" But when you reply, they will say, "Unfortunately we are busy." They are not against an invitation, they are not against God, they are merely at that stage of life when they are busy.

Then there are those people who are at eleven o'clock on the clock face. They are so close to accepting an invitation, but not quite yet: "No, I don't think so… but feel free to ask me again some other time."

As you go inviting, you will meet all these people along the clock face, and variations on the way, but your invitation will move them round the clock face towards a relationship with God. No invitation returns void – even if that is not always obvious. Sometimes we may think someone has moved backwards round the clock, anticlockwise, but we can rely on God to be challenging them in their relationship with him.

There is a passage in the Acts of the Apostles where Paul goes to preach the good news to King Agrippa. I wonder where Agrippa was on the invitation clock.

> *Then Agrippa said to Paul, "Do you think that in such a short time you can persuade me to be a Christian?" (Acts 26:8)*

Where might we put Agrippa in the "innovation adoption cycle"? Was he a laggard, a person who makes slow progress and falls behind others? Was he in the late majority – this, so marketers tell us, accounts for roughly 34 per cent of the population; they will adopt a new idea only after seeing that the majority of the population already has. Or was he in the early majority? This also tends to be roughly 34 per cent of the population; these will adopt a new idea after seeing it used successfully by "innovators" and "early adopters" that they know personally. I am not so sure he was an early adopter – unlike Paul, who had faced a high level of risk before the "idea" had been perfected; Paul was the archetypal innovator.

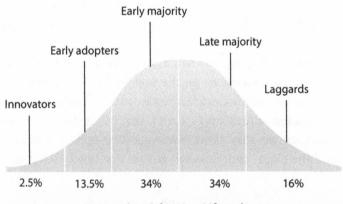

**Innovation Adoption Lifecycle**

Seth Godin has brought to the world's attention the Japanese word *otaku*.[48] *Otaku* is to be fascinated even to the extreme of obsession. Innovators and early adopters are obsessed about something. Godin says that if we don't have an early-adopter constituency for our idea, it won't work. We need to find the people who are listening, and maybe they'll tell their friends. Cornelius the centurion in Acts 10 was *otaku* – we are told he was God-fearing and open to Peter's message. Whenever the apostle Paul went to a new town he went to find the people who were open to his message. Jesus taught us to find the people of peace.

## Rejection within God's purpose

God got turned down nine times by Pharaoh, as through Moses God invited the Egyptian king to let the people go. But fascinatingly, it was God who caused the rejection of the invitation. The plagues were needed to convince Israel, not Pharaoh. Once convinced, they followed Moses into the wilderness. Nine invitations were turned down… but something was happening.

This tells us God can be behind the rejection of an invitation. Rejection, I believe, is part of an ongoing conversation between God and the invited. God brings the heart of the invited person to the surface, so that they might see their heart in the light. Perhaps God was doing that over and over again with Saul, the persecutor of Christians, until one day Saul was truly awakened and convicted very suddenly on the road to Damascus. How many times before that did Saul turn God down?

The sower goes out to sow the seed. Many individual seeds are sown, of course. Some fall on the path, and the birds come and eat the seed. We ourselves today have got nowhere near the good soil in this story (see Matthew 13; Mark 4; Luke 8).

There is a law of averages at work which means that when we do something often enough, we get a certain level of results. There is a ratio between effort and results. We can see this working in all types of sport, when we judge the best player. We see them working on their strengths and especially their weaknesses, to improve their ratio. There is a wonderful verse in Proverbs which says:

> *A gift opens the way and ushers the giver into the*
> *presence of the great. (Proverbs 18:16)*

If you work on your gifts, they will make room for you. As you hone your God-given talent, you get better, and your ratio improves. Instead of one out of ten, you might improve to two out of ten. But it will never be ten out of ten. Not even Jesus got that!

Only one of the twelve disciples asked to walk on water with Jesus. Only one of ten healed lepers came back to thank Jesus.

Results don't come the first time you go round the block:

> *Now the gates of Jericho were securely barred because*
> *of the Israelites. No one went out and no one came in.*
> *Then the Lord said to Joshua, "See, I have delivered*
> *Jericho into your hands, along with its king and its fighting*
> *men. March around the city once with all the armed men.*
> *Do this for six days. Have seven priests carry trumpets of*
> *rams' horns in front of the ark. On the seventh day, march*
> *around the city seven times, with the priests blowing the*
> *trumpets. When you hear them sound a long blast on the*
> *trumpets, make the whole army give a loud shout; then*
> *the wall of the city will collapse and the army will go up,*
> *everyone straight in." (Joshua 6:1–5)*

They had to walk around the wall twelve times before, on the thirteenth occasion, God produced the result. How many times are you prepared to invite someone without seeing a result? Once, twice, ten times, or until their walls of resistance fall down?

C. S. Lewis received *over 800 rejections* before he sold a single piece of writing. If he had given up, there would have been no *Chronicles of Narnia*! I think we need to choose between rejection or regret. By avoiding rejection you experience regret over nothing accomplished. Therefore we need to set some "no" goals – "yes" is the destination, but "no" is how we get there.

Look at Noah. Here are his three main results.

- One hundred and twenty years preaching, and no converts!
- One hundred and twenty years building a ship, and no water to float it!
- One hundred and twenty years warning people that God is about to destroy them, and no flood!

Like Noah, like C. S. Lewis, we must learn to live in the gap of our current reality and desires.

Rejection, I believe, is also part of an ongoing conversation with the inviter and God. I have frequently thought that ministry would be great if it weren't for the people. (How often I have felt that, after a seminar when somebody has complained about what I have said!) But the truth is, I have learned most through complaints.

This is not unusual. At the Red Sea, the children of Israel complained to Moses. Moses was inviting them to have faith in God. Moses had one ear to the people and then, after the complaints, he cried out to God. He used a pattern of aloneness with God in a rhythmic way. He experienced something with the Israelites and went straight to God. We too need to go into God's presence on behalf of people who reject us. Perhaps as inviters this can become our ultimate orientating reality. We hear a rejection, we go to God; we hear a harsh word, we go to God; we see someone respond, we go to God. Moses eventually desired to go to God so much that God showed him his glory:

*There is a place near me where you may stand on a rock. (Exodus 33:21)*

For the serial inviter, being near to God is our greatest good. In the end, Moses didn't need the Promised Land of Canaan any more, because God had become the place he wanted to go.

God blessed me with thinking partners who were not echo chambers. They came in the guise of church leaders who dared to disagree with me. When I took the trouble to revisit the area of disagreement, I could find a new pathway with God.

*You will seek me and find me when you seek me with all your heart. (Jeremiah 29:13)*

We can learn lessons from nature: there is a season to sow and a season to reap – you don't do both for the same crop in the same season. We don't know the season of reaping, but we do know the season of sowing. Every farmer knows that you don't plant a seed one day and then come back the next and ask where it is! Farmers plant in faith and hope. They have faith because they can see the harvest in advance, in their mind's eye; while they hope because they cannot control the weather. But we get so frustrated when our missional activity does not result in a positive outcome immediately.

In farming and in life generally, there is a gestation period. The gestation period for a human baby is 266 days. For rabbits it is a little less and for elephants it is quite a bit more. We don't

114

know the gestation period here, and in our microwave culture we find it difficult to wait for anything. Everything that has to do with long-term rewards with short-term sacrifices is difficult for us.

This surely is the antidote to the disappointment over the negative response of a friend. Invitational patience is learning to handle the passing of time. We need to know when people simply need more time. Patience helps us to remain alert for the next opportunity to invite. Patience also enables us to keep getting ready to invite, by learning how to get better at overcoming any fear. Patience allows us to take little setbacks in our stride. Patience allows us to wait on the decisions of those we have invited. And patience allows us to take a break from time to time, because we know the fruit of invitation is in God's hand.

David fled from Saul for many years before eventually being crowned king. Abraham waited twenty-five years for the birth of Isaac. Abraham was promised a land and 400 years later it still had not quite come to fruition.

As James said:

> Be patient, then, brothers and sisters, until the Lord's coming. See how the farmer waits for the land to yield its valuable crop, patiently waiting for the autumn and spring rains. (James 5:7)

## No sowing – no reaping

But strangely there is another problem associated with learning lessons from nature in Western Christianity: we attempt to reap what we have not sown. Bev Shepherd in her book *Insight into Stress* says:

*We often live as if there is only one season-harvest. We attempt to reap what we have not sown.*[49]

Can you imagine if a farmer had not planted a crop and we found the farmer in a field at harvest-time, day after day, disappointed over the lack of harvest? We would have to explain to the farmer that there had been no planting in the spring.

If we are not reaping, have we sown? Have we made invitations; have we had God-conversations; have we nourished relationships to such an extent that we might have the possibility of a harvest? The research I have conducted says we are sadly lacking in the planting of a crop of invitations. Why can't we live in the season of spring for a while?

Let's learn the lessons of a farmer. God says, "If you plant the seed, I will grow it." You really can't get a better deal than that. When it didn't look like anything was happening… it was! The seed must be planted with no immediate expectation of the harvest.

## What's happening under the surface?

Holy Saturday might be another example of when it didn't look like anything was happening. Eugene Peterson says in his book *Under the Unpredictable Plant*:[50]

*Holy Saturday, the next-to-last event in the eight-day week, is virtually ignored. It is the most undercelebrated event of Jesus' life. Holy Saturday: confinement turns into concentration, illusion transmutes into hope, death changes to resurrection.*

This way of living is so countercultural. Just because someone rejects an invitation does not mean that nothing is happening!

The emotion of fear when thinking of inviting people can build up a feeling of pressure. This pressure is a worried feeling that you get when you have to deal with a difficult or complicated situation. It is really difficult to think rationally when under a feeling of pressure. Sir Clive Woodward, manager of England's successful Rugby World Cup team, used teacups as an analogy. When under pressure, think of a teacup, T-CUP. Pause, and breathe:

*T – Thinking*

*C – Clearly*

*U – Under*

*P – Pressure*

Think of a teacup and then think "God is with us". That is clear thinking under pressure!

## The power of a story

We need to focus on stories in becoming better inviters. We don't pay enough attention nowadays to the importance of sharing personal stories as we communicate with people. We have stories of people in our congregations who overcome obstacles, who face their fears. We need to learn how to make our stories more compelling.

I believe we should always carry two books with us, the book we are reading and the book we are writing. There is nothing better than carrying a Bible with us. But for our stories we also need to carry a journal so that we can write down our stories and remember what God has been doing in our lives. As we tell compelling stories we can help people see a different vision for themselves. This will make our invitation more powerful.

## What motivates you?

What if I invite someone and they say no? What if I invite someone and they not only say no, but they ask me a difficult question?

These are fear-based questions. We are foreseeing the worst consequences of the invitation. Let me help you change your paradigm for a moment. What if I gave you £1,000 for every invite? Would you get motivated? Who would you talk to? What would you say to them and what would you do if they said no? The idea of changing your vision will change the outcome and purge the fear. Now, ask yourself what vision of God – rather than £1,000 – would change your vision to invite?

## Aren't you even curious?

There are not many people who can say, "I came out of the womb. I didn't cry but I invited my first person straight away!" or "I was in nursery. I was already inviting my fellow toddlers." The truth is, most of us are afraid of inviting. We fear what we don't know anything about. But when we get knowledge and skills, fear disappears.

Now, a way to make fear dissipate is to develop a deep curiosity in the thing we fear. This will give us knowledge of the unknown – and then we take action.

## Learn to lament

Fear grows strongest when we allow it to fester in a wordless darkness. To speak out fear to another begins to loosen the grip fear has on us. To make fear take form in speech is to name it as something that can be confronted – not on our own but in the community of those willing to speak their fears aloud and thus begin to subdue them. The psalms of lament (e.g. Psalms 13 and 86) allow us to give voice together to our fears and anxieties.

## Let grace be your teacher

There is a line in the hymn "Amazing Grace" which gives hope to all us fledgling inviters.

> *'Twas grace that taught my heart to fear and grace my fears relieved.*

It is clear that John Newton (1725–1807), the hymn-writer, believed in the need to be taught to fear well, and that only grace could give the courage to fear as we should. Then that same grace of God goes on to relieve our fears. Grace makes sure that fears will not rule us. Grace puts fear in its place.

## Living in the discomfort zone

It can feel like a long way from our comfort zone to a discomfort zone. It is like making a quantum leap, described in the dictionary as "a sudden highly significant advance; a breakthrough" (Collins). I would suggest that we do something each day that widens our invitational comfort zone.

Each of us has a comfort zone. Each time I venture out, to stretch my capability with God, to take new risks, I find the edge of the comfort zone highlighted by fear. I used to wait for the fear to go away before I took a chance. Now I don't. I now know that you have to take the fear with you alongside your courage. The Hebrew word *shalom* implies more than an absence of violence and conflict. It means well-being, health, security, and rest. When we deal with our fears, we are dealing with a major barrier to finding *shalom*. The initiative for reconciliation with God comes from God. That is why, when God calls us, our fears are revealed ... so that, with God, we can take action to remove those fears.

It is said that a journey of a thousand miles begins with one step. But not all steps are created equal. Many Christians want to become missional and reach their friends for Christ, but it is the first step that does them in. It is only as they take the first step that their fears are exposed as a complete fraud and that they discover their imagination had become disordered. The first step – before anyone else in the world believes it – is that you have to believe it.

In Joshua 3 we see that the priests had to step into the water with the ark of the covenant before the waters began to part. Until they took the step, the waters did not move.

## Pushing through the "Oh help" moment

Two of my favourite cartoon characters are Scooby Doo and his companion, Shaggy. They were always getting themselves into scary situations. Scooby is famous for a gulp. A gulp is an indication of an involuntary fear reaction. In many cartoons, Shaggy says, "Like, whatever you do, Scoob, don't look down." In each episode there is always something to be overcome and a gulp, which is why those of us who like Scooby Doo enjoy them so much. They manage to overcome the situation together. In mission there can be times when we inwardly gulp at what God is asking us to do.

During the call of Moses at the burning bush, in Moses' reluctance to do what God is calling him to do, he says this:

*"What if they do not believe me or listen to me and say,
'The Lord did not appear to you'?" (Exodus 4:1)*

God responds by asking Moses what was in his hand. Moses
is carrying his staff, a wooden stick which he used in tending
sheep, as well as giving himself greater stability as he walked in
the desert. God proceeds to tell Moses to let go of it – to throw it
down. Moses throws down his staff and when it hits the ground
it turns into a snake. One thing you can be certain of: a shepherd
in the desert, like Moses, knew snakes. So he starts to run from
it – he no longer has his staff to defend himself. But the Lord tells
Moses to pick up the snake by the tail.

This is the "Oh help" moment. Moses would know that the
last way to pick up a snake is by the tail; it could curl up and bite
you. Normally he would use his staff to pin it to the ground by the
back of the neck, and pick it up there, so that it could not twist
and curl and bite. Fearfully, Moses obeyed and took hold of the
snake by the tail. When he got his fingers wrapped around the
snake it changed back into a staff right in the palm of his hand.

Very often there is an "Oh help" moment as we invite. This is
when we need to summon up our courage to face the possibility
of rejection.

We are all of us failures – at least, the best of us are.

*Only those who will risk going too far can possibly find
out how far one can go. (T. S. Eliot)*[51]

## An audience of one

Moses experienced what all leaders ultimately fear: rejection by
the people they are called to lead. When he killed the Egyptian
soldier, and then several times in the wilderness, his leadership
was sorely tested. Aaron compromised his leadership by building

a golden calf. But Moses played to an audience of one alone. How easy it is for all of us to play to our friends, rather than to God. When we resist God's prompting and follow the crowd, the heart is stunted by lack of courage.

We have an unnoticed inheritance. We may want to be part of a big church without contributing beyond our presence and our credit card. Perhaps we remember times when our churches were packed out; when tent missions or stadium events seemed the way to bring people in. We can so easily be drawn into wanting big successful events. While these events were important, we need also to think small: the narrow road is one person wide. The stories of the lost coin or the lost sheep emphasize the importance of each single individual to God.

As Luke says:

> Whoever can be trusted with very little can also be trusted with much, and whoever is dishonest with very little will also be dishonest with much. (Luke 16:10)

## Seek clarification

Sometimes we don't invite because we fear the difficult questions that may follow. But we should not hesitate to offer clarification if we think someone does not understand something. This can deepen the conversation and quite possibly increase the likelihood of a positive result – if not this time, maybe later, after the person has had time to think some more.

## Remember you are dust

Co-founder of Apple, Steve Jobs, in the months before he died, said something which might be helpful to some of as we face our fears. It is about living each day as if it is your last on earth.

*Remembering that I'll be dead soon is the most important tool I've ever encountered to help me make the big choices in life. Because almost everything – all external expectations, all pride, all fear of embarrassment or failure – these things just fall away in the face of death, leaving only what is truly important. Remembering that you are going to die is the best way I know to avoid the trap of thinking you have something to lose. You are already naked. There is no reason not to follow your heart.*[52]

## Look beyond the fear

We need to be developing practices of facing fear as we attempt to respond to the mission of God.

- Step 1 – breathe deeply. Fritz Perls said, "Fear is excitement without the breath."[53]
- Step 2 – reverse your desire. Quit looking at fear as limiting. Good things lie on the other side of the fear.
- Step 3 – optimize your hope. What would I do if I believed Immanuel my God is with me? Then go and do it.

## Learn to fail well

Failing well is one of the Christian life's most crucial skills, but it is rarely taught. Success and failure are not polar opposites: you often need to endure the second to enjoy the first. Failure can indeed be a better teacher than success. It can also be a sign of creativity. The best way to avoid short-term failure is to keep churning out the same old things.

Michael Jordan, the legendary basketball player, said this about failing well:

> *I've missed more than 9000 shots in my career. I've lost almost 300 games, 26 times, I've been trusted to take the game winning shot and missed. I've failed over and over and over again in my life. And that is why I succeed.*[54]

The psalms give us a clue on how to fail well.

> *Whom have I in heaven but you? And earth has nothing I desire besides you. My flesh and my heart may fail, but God is the strength of my heart and my portion for ever. (Psalm 73:25–26)*

One of the things failure teaches us is dependence on God.

## Bring your fear into God's presence

When fear strikes, breathe and relax. Use contemplation. The word "contemplate" is based on *templum*, a place for observation. For us that means not simply to observe but to reflect on these things in the presence of God. Fear comes as a fully formed story with what will happen next. We need to read our fears in God's presence.

## Face the challenge

In the Garden of Gethsemane, Jesus faced his fear. How did he do it? And can we learn from that how better to face our own challenges in life? I see five principles.

First, he involved his friends. He had his closest companions with him – Peter, James and John.

Second, he expressed emotion: "he began to be sorrowful and troubled" (Matthew 26:37).

Third, he coped actively by petitioning his Father.

Fourth, he altered his perception: "Take this cup away, but if not – your will be done."

Fifth, he faced his fear as he said to his disciples, "Rise! Let us go! Here comes my betrayer!" (Matthew 26:46)

Now, if we reverse the order, we can see how Jesus F-A-C-E-S a challenge:

**F**ace rather than flee the fear.

**A**lter your perception.

**C**ope actively by praying.

**E**xpress emotion.

**S**ocial support through friends.

# 6

## Best Practice

Much of the invitation process is completely invisible and therefore we do not notice it. And what we don't notice we won't change.

A church leader announces a future event and asks congregation members to invite someone. The next thing to get noticed in the process is the event itself, and whether any guests have actually been invited by the congregation. Based on this evidence alone we make decisions about the effectiveness of mission.

We fail to notice if anyone has asked God, or whether people have been prompted to invite someone, whether someone has the courage to invite, or what happens during the invitation itself.

Therefore let me introduce you to the acronym ACORN. I have chosen this word because, for an oak tree to live, the acorn must be buried in the ground and die. For an invitation to take place, we must take our fear with us and invite someone, and as we invite them that fear dies.

ACORN will help us to track invitation and give us some new metrics to make us more aware of the activity of God in the life of the church.

## A is for Ask

When it comes to inviting, asking is the beginning of receiving. Receiving is not the problem – it is our failure to ask. Receiving is like the sand on the seashore – there is plenty of it, but we need to select our part of the beach. Then, once we have defined whom we want to invite, we ask with simple faith. We make plans to invite like an adult and believe in our invitation like a child. You won't get everything you want in asking. Nothing in life works like that. We are likely from time to time to get rain on our parade.

Faith operates in the domain of things the physical eye cannot see, but it is able to see the invisible. Faith knows the unknowable, hears the inaudible and touches the intangible. By faith… who does God bring to mind when we think about invitation? Who is in your proximity? Who is in your network of contacts? Who is on God's heart? Who is on yours?

## C is for the Call of God

God called Abraham; God called Moses; Jesus called four disciples by name. Saul was called on the road to Damascus. The Hebrew word for Bible is *miqra*, a noun formed from the verb *qara*, to call. The Bible is not a book to carry around and read for information on God, but a voice to listen to. "… go and make disciples" (Matthew 28:19).

In Genesis 12:4 it says, "So Abram went, as the Lord had told him". Abraham was called, and he obeyed. There is no hint of hesitation, talking about it, ruminating, or delay; when he was called to go out, he went out. "… many are called, but few are chosen" (Matthew 22:14, KJV). Jesus is basically saying, "I called and you refused." Such calls come again and again to many, but we turn a deaf ear to them; that's when we show ourselves to be hearers only, and not doers of the word.

We have seen that the Bible is full of illustrations of God calling and prodding people into service in spite of their overwhelming sense of inadequacy. They were thrust into ministry environments almost against their wills. Jesus too was constantly stretching the disciples' faith. In the story of the feeding of the 5,000, Jesus said to the disciples:

> *They do not need to go away. You give them something to eat. (Matthew 14:16)*

It was a test of their faith. Like us, the disciples made excuses and told Jesus things he already knew. "We have here only five loaves of bread and two fish..." Jesus responded, "Bring them here to me" (Matthew 14:17–18). In other words, "Just bring what you have and I'll work with that." When we do that, we experience Immanuel God with us – however inadequate we may feel about the process. For God says:

> *"I have called you by name, you are mine." (Isaiah 43:1, ESV)*

God is still calling today, as he did with Isaiah. "Whom shall I send?" (Isaiah 6:8). The reason he calls is that there is work to be done. So this is an invitation to enter into what God is doing and intending to get done in the world. We have to be intentional in our daily response: "Here am I. Send me!" (see Isaiah 6:8). We accept God's invitation. God's call is spoken as a question, inviting a response; we have the freedom of a yes or a no. It is never a matter of coercion. We are invited into God's work.

But we can turn down God's invitation. In the parable of the sower we perhaps fail to appreciate how scandalized we would actually be if a farmer scattered seed in the manner described. What a waste! All that resource which is not being used in an efficient manner. But I think the farmer represents our gracious God who extravagantly calls us to become who we are meant to be. Despite our lack of response, God keeps on giving us opportunities by scattering the seed.

Recently I purchased a new cordless phone for home. It has over sixty possible ringtones. Wouldn't it be good if we had a way of identifying the call of God in our lives? The problem is that God has different calling patterns. For Joseph it was dreams, for Moses it was a burning bush, for Nehemiah it was a report, for Saul it was a blinding light, for countless others it was the incidents of their lives.

By faith, who is God calling you to invite? Is there a name or a face that pops into your mind as you read this question?

## The invitational cross

We can ask ourselves this question in an act of worship, as we seek to hear his call. One way that has proved successful is to write the initials of the person God is asking you to invite on a piece of paper, and then pin it on to a cross. When everyone has done this we can see God's unique mission field right across the congregation.

Invitation cross first used in the Anglican chaplaincy in Limeuil, France.

I have seen unique mission fields created using names written on paper – from sunflower leaves to stick-on starfish on a beach.

## O is for Obey

Currently in the life of the church we recognize and reward success rather than obedience. So, when I ask church leaders around the world how they know what's happening with invitation, they tell me that they judge by how many new faces they see on a Sunday morning. I might call these the invitations that resulted in a yes.

The invitations that resulted in a no, but were also prompted by God, remain invisible. Congregation members who get a no are therefore not given the same accolade as those who get a yes. This means we are rewarding success rather than obedience. Jesus said, "[Teach] them to obey everything I have commanded you" (Matthew 28:20).

One of the speakers I loved to listen to when I was in my early twenties was Alan Redpath. He described the Christian life as an "in and out" life:

> In with God for orders, out for God with obedience. In with God for worship, out for God in mission. In with God for surrender, out for God in service.[55]

In the landscape of invitation, Jesus calls us to walk on water. When Simon Peter stepped out of the boat, he obeyed the prompting of Christ. This is what happens in invitation. Jesus prompts us to invite someone and we have to walk towards that prompting. It is a type of walking on water. We can be afraid of sinking, but we must keep our eyes on Jesus, for he is calling us towards him. And whether we sink or not, Jesus is there to hold us and embrace us. He surrounds us and is beside us.

God is calling us to participate in something bigger than ourselves. Participation is one of the key moves of God in our generation. Marathons, fun runs, cycling, and other activities for charity are hugely popular. This present generation has to cope with multiple things happening at once, which has a shrinking effect on attention spans. Maybe they will not be so good at joining things and becoming members, but they will be good at short-term participation. This may be how they obey the call to help others.

So are you going to participate in the call of God in your life?

## R is for Reporting results

We allow perceived failure to deflate us. We suddenly lose confidence and become dispirited. When Peter denied Jesus, he was crushed and inwardly destroyed. Matthew 26:75 says "he went outside and wept bitterly". It is hard to envision the depth of the emotional low Peter experienced that weekend, as Jesus was crucified and buried in a tomb just outside Jerusalem. Every Christian who dares to grow and mature in Jesus will face a moment when the cock will crow. But this result in Peter's life led to maturity, as Jesus restored him (John 21:15–19). In fact, Simon Peter's report has helped countless others down the generations.

Results need to be shared – even when we think they reflect badly on us.

I have friends in France whose house is called *La Coursonne*. This name refers to the buds which are left on the vine when the vineyard owner has pruned it back. From the buds growth comes, and the growth is even stronger because all the unnecessary part of the vine has been cut away. Pruning is a very painful process.

> *I am the true vine, and my Father is the gardener. He cuts off every branch in me that bears no fruit, while every branch that does bear fruit he prunes so that it will be even more fruitful. (John 15:2)*

Serial inviters know what it is to be pruned. The pain of hearing a no on a repeated basis is part of the pruning process. But this is how the fruit of patience is cultivated.

Of course, all of this needs to be learned and experienced. We need to teach our newer Christians that God may well test their faith. The new Christian often starts well, in that honeymoon period of first love for God, and starts inviting. Have you ever puzzled why they stop? We have created a church culture where we are afraid to expose doubts and fear. Our new honeymoon Christian's liberation to invite soon moves into a slavery of conformity to the uniformity where no one invites; no one wants to expose their vulnerabilities in mission.

Those of us working for the extension of the kingdom of God will never see the full results of our work. It is as though we are planting sequoias. The redwood forests are the remains of the virgin sequoia forest. These trees have a lifespan of over 2,000 years. And so we are in a long line of disciples who have made disciples, who have made disciples, and so on, over 2,000 years. But there are interim results, and these should be shared.

How might we do that?

## *On assignment – learning dyads*

In soccer it used to be that goalscorers were the most valuable members of the team, but in 1986 all that began to change. Goalscorers now share the limelight with another key element in the process, that is, the player who provides the assist. An assist is a contribution by a player which helps to score a goal. Most commonly, this is credited to a player for passing or crossing the ball to the scorer, but it may also be awarded to a player whose shot rebounds (off a defender, goalkeeper, or goalpost) to a teammate who scores; or to a player who wins a penalty kick for another player to convert.

In invitation we often focus on the invited person, but we must not forget the inviter. This is the one who plays a vital role in the invitation process by assisting with an invite. So also in invitation we need to start reporting the results from the inviter as well as the invited person.

One of the most effective ways I have found for supporting obedience to a call is the power of assignment and the formation of learning dyads.

We have been taught in our schools not to copy the work of others because that is cheating. Outside our schooling system, copying is called collaboration. The problem is, trial and error, and especially copying others have become stigmatized ways of learning. But I have found great effectiveness in working in pairs (dyads) to try things out – both copying, and trial and error. Once again, the assist comes alongside the goalscorer.

The story of Moses begins when Pharaoh commands the Hebrew midwives to kill all the male Israelite babies. Two women said no. That took courage. Where did it come from? It says, because they "feared God" (Exodus 1:17). They had a strong sense that while there was a pharaoh, there was a God over Pharaoh, and while they must give account to the authorities of Egypt, they must also give account to one over all human authorities. They feared God and they said no. This is where their courage came from – from the belief that God honours us when we obey, and has our good at heart. And so they acted rightly.

Now there were two midwives, and I think it's possible that a great part of their belief and courage came from the fact that they stood alongside each other. Shiphrah had Puah. Puah had Shiphrah. And when they were threatened, they could say, "Well, at least when we go before the king of Egypt, we will not be alone; we have each other." We need companions – companions of conviction and faith and courage, who can help us do what God calls us to do.

Leaders should not fear to give their people assignments.

> *"I want you to do this, and when you are done, get back to me."*

> *"I want you to go and invite some people and call me back."*

These assignments need to be achievable, of course. And better that they be able to do them quite quickly, so that they can get back to you and soon get on with the next one. This is like leaving little bread crumbs on the way to the treasure. Assignments are a great tool, so that we do not ignore the performance of people. I believe that if you give your best to the few in developing their walk with God through assignments, the many will soon follow.

Assignments can be given on an individual basis within the congregation, but I am suggesting the establishment of learning dyads. An invitational learning dyad is two people working together to become invitational. The fear of failure at invitation would not be so great if failure were not so harshly looked upon by others. Fear of the material consequences of failure is compounded by fear of the unsympathetic attitude of the church. The church may not go as far as the world and say that the person is a loser, but it comes quite close by offering little sympathy and support. A learning partnership, as in the learning dyad, offers that support. Each shares with the other who they are going to invite. And after the invitation has taken place, they can immediately report the result to each other.

The other major benefit of a learning dyad is to combat something called loss aversion. It is a very powerful fear that is described in the English proverb "A bird in the hand is worth two in the bush". This recalls the proverb in Ecclesiastes:

> *... a living dog is better than a dead lion. (Ecclesiastes 9:4, ESV)*

In other words, it's better to have a lesser but certain advantage than the possibility of a greater one that may come to nothing. This is a fear of future regret. In the twelve common reasons, it was expressed in these three:

- What if it damages my friendship?
- I fear the congregation will think my friend is not "our" type of person.
- I don't want to be seen as strange.

The possibility of losing a friend, the possibility of losing the respect of the congregation, the possibility of appearing strange and losing credibility... these are all greater in the eyes of such people than the possibility of someone coming to faith in Jesus Christ.

Nobel Prize winner Daniel Kahneman calls this loss aversion. He says:

*We typically fear loss twice as much as we relish success.*[56]

Loss aversion is a concern which is completely out of proportion about small, certain losses, or an over-the-top sensitivity to small losses or small failures. If you get very disturbed with a small loss, you are not likely to try things. We are generally delighted when we win, but distressed when we lose. Here is an example:

- You win a competition and the prize is a choice between two options – to either receive a guaranteed payout of £90, or to take a 90 per cent chance of getting a £100 payout, but with a 10 per cent chance of receiving nothing.
- You are fined and given a choice between two options – to either pay £90 outright, or to take a 10 per cent chance of paying nothing but with a 90 per cent chance of having to pay £100.

Which of these two scenarios would you choose?

Loss aversion theory has found that the overwhelming majority of people will choose to receive the cast-iron guaranteed £90 as outlined in scenario one, and they will bet for a chance to pay nothing in scenario two. This is inconsistent and illogical behaviour: for the same £90 payout, people refuse the bet when there is a gain but accept it when there is a loss. We decide on taking a risk or being safe simply because of the perception of gain or loss.

One of the reasons we don't invite is that we might lose a friend. Jesus tackles our loss aversion:

> *For whoever wants to save their life will lose it, but whoever loses their life for me will find it. (Matthew 16:25)*

Paul said:

> *For to me, to live is Christ and to die is gain. (Philippians 1:21)*

Martin Luther King said:

> *The true revolutionary is one who has nothing to lose.* [57]

In Mark 14:7 we read:

> *... trouble or persecution comes because of the word*

And Jesus said:

> *Anyone who loves their father or mother more than me is not worthy of me; anyone who loves their son or daughter more than me is not worthy of me. Whoever does not take up their cross and follow me is not worthy of me. Whoever finds their life will lose it, and whoever loses their life for my sake will find it.*
> *(Matthew 10:37–39)*

At some point in time we need to die to who we are, in order to give birth to who we can become.

In the learning dyad we can learn to tackle things by working with our learning partner, and as the fear of loss comes up in invitational mission we can ask what it is that we are afraid of losing. We can ascertain whether we are seeing the whole picture. When we attempt to see beyond the fear, we are better able to recognize if we are keeping ourselves stuck, and if we would benefit from letting go of what we think we need. When loss aversion comes up we can look for the alternative of seeking after God. This gives us a regular assessment of our intentions and motivations. It has the potential of changing how we see the inevitability of loss. The reality is that loss *is* inevitable. Our learning partner will be a good sounding board and will provide that accountability to help us obey the nudge of God.

Most people who start a project begin with a fair amount of fear, uncertainty, and anxiety, acknowledging the possibility of failure. With inviting, we are very vulnerable because we are venturing on an initiative. There isn't so much to lose in the beginning. But then we build something substantial – and we do have a lot to lose! At that point we are not as able to move through fear and uncertainty as we were in the beginning. We don't trust in the process that brought growth. We start to trust in the product of the process. To grow you need to be really comfortable in being uncomfortable. Then you'll be given a series of God-given opportunities brilliantly disguised as problems and challenges.

There are times when we need to assess how we are doing in making disciples, so let's check the numbers.

- How many invitations have been offered in the last quarter?

- How many visitors have stayed in the last quarter?
- How many people in your congregation have moved on in their relationship with God?

What's your answer to those questions? If you find it hard to reply, then now is a good time to start the reporting process.

In the appendix, you will find a suggestion for a reporting mechanism in the process of invitation.

## N is for Numinous

The numinous is an almost tangible sense of the presence of God. In his book *The Idea of the Holy*, German theologian Rudolph Otto describes it with three Latin words:

> *The numinous is a mystery (mysterium) that is both terrifying (tremendum) and fascinating (fascinans) at the same time.*[58]

So in the asking and the call within ACORN, did you hear the call of God? Did you feel the presence of God as you obeyed? Can you see the work of God in the results? Is the fruit of the Spirit visible in the report? The more we can help Christians to find God's presence in the activity of mission, the more I believe we will seek the presence of God.

One night on his travels, Paul heard God speak to him in a vision:

> *... many people in this city belong to me. (Acts 18:10, NLT)*

The idea of God being already at work – even on particular people – before we go and invite is, in my experience, absolutely real. It is the hidden reality of the presence of God in our societies that God is more active behind our backs than in front of our faces.

So we should join God in mission and find these people and unite them to other believers in the area.

## Become the chief inviter

In order to help congregation members overcome a fear of inviting, I ask church leaders to individually invite congregation members to invite their friends, and then say to them, "Blame me." In other words: say the church leader has asked you to invite your friend so you really had no choice.

Sometimes we have to carry a burden for others in this way. The boy David as a shepherd provided protection for those under his charge. Jesus went on to say that he was the good shepherd who would lay down his life for the sheep. It is an image intended to inspire the faith of disciples in difficult times.

So church leaders must not only invite their congregation members to invite, but they themselves are to become the chief inviters. They should be constantly looking for people whom God wants us to invite. They should also model all aspects of invitational experience. For example: "I invited John on Tuesday. John said no!" We will know when we have got invitation into the life of the church, when the church can say, "Well done for inviting: the result is up to God."

## Research the outskirts

God will already be drawing people into the vicinity of the church (both building and people). Form an invitational committee and start to plot out who is coming in and out of our buildings, in and out of our meetings. Who is dropping off children for activities? Who have we not seen for some time? Who has had weddings, attended funerals or baptisms, that might be personally invited?

## Script the critical moves

When I finish reading the book of Acts I say to myself, "No wonder!" No wonder Christianity burst forth – just look what they did! It is obvious after reading the book that faith uninvested in labour is wasted. "… faith without works is dead" (James 2:20, NKJV). They invited people and shared their faith. The early Christians invested their belief in activity.

In my earlier book, *Unlocking the Growth*, I answer in nine words the question asked by many who have not invited for a long time: "What would I say?"

> *"Would you like to come to church with me?"*

Also work through with congregation members the other question:

> *"What are we inviting people to?"*

Just make it as simple as possible.

## Don't just announce – encourage!

We have fallen for the myth that people act rationally at all times and have the benefit of "perfect information". In reality, people are happy to stick with what they've got as long as it's adequate: their behaviour is more about routines and rules of thumb. And inertia sets in due to both the cost of acquiring new information and the cost of switching.

Therefore we can no longer simply announce an invitational event and leave things there. Now that we know that people are afraid, announcement alone just will not do. We now need to move our leadership style to announcement and encouragement. Congregation members need encouragement and protection to move in invitation. Invitation makes them feel exposed. So we must encourage – whether that comes through getting them to blame the chief inviter (as detailed above), or reminding them that the yes and the no of an invitation belong to God, or sharing stories of invitation, both the yeses and the noes.

## Celebrate faithfulness

Life is difficult for everyone, Christian and non-Christian alike. Having faith in God doesn't mean you won't have problems. If anything, being a Christian means more troubles. This is for two primary reasons.

- You are asked to die to your own selfish desires and live for God on his terms.
- You will be persecuted for standing up for Christ by a world that rejects him.

Therefore faithfulness needs to be recognized and encouraged.

The formula for faithfulness and failure in invitational mission is three words long. For failure, it is simply: could–should–don't. We could invite, we should invite, but we don't invite. For faithfulness, the formula is equally simple and understandable – it just has one word different from the failure formula: could–should–do.

We need to appreciate and celebrate faithfulness. The more we celebrate it, the more invitation will happen. Make it obvious in public worship that you value faithfulness over success. At the moment there is no incentive to publish bad news in today's church, but consider this short selection of testimonies of faithfulness given by Luke in Acts.

- Peter and John are tried by the ruling council of the Jews. (Acts 4)
- They are again taken into custody for trial and are released after being flogged. (Acts 5)
- The persecution, trial, and murder of Stephen sets the stage for an all-out persecution of the church in Jerusalem by the ruling council of the Jews. (Acts 6)
- Herod kills John's brother, James, and persecutes Peter. (Acts 12)
- Unbelieving Jews in Antioch instigate a persecution and drive out Paul and Barnabas. (Acts 13)

In all these examples we find faithfulness rather than obvious success.

## Find your serial inviters

Invariably there seems to be in each congregation 5 per cent of people who have no trouble inviting. These I have called serial inviters. The role of the serial inviter is not well known in the church, but most churches have one. They do most of the inviting in the church, they get rejected the most – by those outside and inside the church.

We need to deploy them, to help others overcome their fear of inviting. Christianity is often more caught than taught, and on top of that, many people are not into new ideas, but tend to copy other people.

Colgate toothpaste ran a number of adverts saying that their toothpaste gave people the "ring of confidence" as it made people's breath fresh and teeth extra white. I met a newly ordained vicar who was just getting used to her dog collar, and her colleague called it the "white ring of confidence". People treat you differently when you have one on. But it also gives the person who is wearing it more opportunities and more confidence to invite, because it is expected of them by the general public. So while we have serial inviters, we also have the professional inviters, and we need to make use of them.

I have studied people who are serial inviters and those of us who are not. My conclusion is that those who "overthink" don't always become serial inviters – they see too many risks. The person who starts to invite sees the opportunity, and any fears of failure are swept away by the task. They have what is known as the bumblebee syndrome: aerodynamically speaking, the bumblebee shouldn't be able to fly, but the bumblebee doesn't know that so it goes on flying anyway.

Serial inviters are just like the bumblebee. They don't realize that they could fall flat on their faces. For the rest of us, fear has a knife to our throats. The serial inviter, by contrast, is thinking, "It's worth doing even if I fail." But for the rest of us, we fail by default rather than run the risk of failing as a result of making the effort to invite. It is a mental game for us, we play it out in our minds, we wait until conditions are better; and, of course, they rarely do get better.

But our gracious God has not left us alone with our risks. God is described like an eagle that stirs up its nest and hovers over its young, that spreads its wings to catch them and carries them on its pinions. So the serial inviter might be able to help us run towards our fears and, like a bumblebee, fly with God to become a serial inviter as well.

There is an intriguing beginning to Hebrews 12 which I believe is helpful to all of us who are seeking to become serial inviters.

*Therefore, since we are surrounded by such a great cloud of witnesses, let us throw off everything that hinders and the sin that so easily entangles. And let us run with perseverance the race marked out for us, fixing our eyes on Jesus, the pioneer and perfecter of faith. For the joy set before him he endured the cross, scorning its shame, and sat down at the right hand of the throne of God. Consider him who endured such opposition from sinners, so that you will not grow weary and lose heart. (Hebrews 12:1–3)*

The witnesses referred to are found in the previous chapter. By faith Abraham... by faith Isaac... by faith Jacob... Are they watching us and cheering us on? What a marvellous thought!

## Form an invitational research team

Look at the neighbourhood of your church and start to invite a conversation with the neighbourhood. A good question in the survey would be, "Do you know of anybody who might be interested in being invited to church?" Sometimes the person who is asked that question may point you to someone straightaway, or ponder the question and tell others they meet in the vicinity.

Set a task of finding out what God is already up to among your neighbours, by formulating some questions and tasking a team to do the research.

## Write five reasons not to give up

I meet many conflict-allergic church leaders, afraid to challenge the prevailing culture. I recognize them, because I recognize the same issues in my own walk with God. Many leaders hesitate to introduce anything that adds to the conflict level of their ministries.

Fear and hesitation can result from financial concerns. These represent one of the emasculating dynamics of a salaried church leader. They might lose their job, which means they might not be able to provide for their family. Fear arrests the leader's heart. Vision wastes away. The spirit weakens. Growth stops. The leader dies in place. On the other hand, an invitational leader brings conflict into a congregation by raising the topic of invitation. Then, sadly, just watch the active sabotage in a congregation that will often occur, as the leader encourages going and making disciples. But I say: face the fear of conflict.

In addition, the word of God in your life attracts conflict. In the parable of the sower it says that

> *trouble or persecution comes because of the word*
> *(Mark 4:17)*

Joy follows the experience of the word being challenged as we endure the conflict. Jesus in the end attracted the nails and the wounds by which we are healed. Jesus through conflict is the joy of our salvation.

At some point you will want to give up. So… write down your five reasons why you will not. Best do it now.

# 7

# The Ultimate Inviter

The harvest is plentiful but the inviters are few! So what is this harvest?

The harvest is a hurt world that is very fearful. Fear is endemic in society. As human beings we will never remove fear, but through Christ it need not dominate our lives. We don't have to be regulated by it, motivated by it, or controlled by it.

As human beings we are afraid of people discovering our shame, or inadequacy, or our susceptibility to be wounded and how easily broken we can be. And so we try to control the situation by hiding our real selves.

Perhaps unconsciously we humans fear the reality of death, of having to suffer. We are frightened of being diminished; we fear old age.

There is a social and relational fear of being demoted, not valued, not needed, rejected, ostracized and seen as odd. Many of us remember the nursery rhyme

> *Sticks and stones may break my bones*
> *But words will never hurt me.*

But we all know that wounding words can bring damage that lasts a lifetime.

There is a fear of chaos, fear of having no meaning in life, that it is all a waste of time, that there will be no legacy.

These fears are some of the evidence of humanity searching for God. This is the plentiful harvest.

When human beings are dominated and controlled by fear, we have to find ways out. And addiction is one of the routes – to alcohol, drugs, self-harm, work, gambling, shopping… these are some of today's stress-relievers, the results of fear. Who in our society is not addicted? We are all about soothing, getting something from outside to make ourselves feel OK, temporarily.

Blaise Pascal was a philosopher in the seventeenth century. He wrote:

*What else does this craving, and this helplessness,*
*proclaim but that there was once in man a true*
*happiness, of which all that now remains is the*
*empty print and trace? This he tries in vain to fill with*
*everything around him, seeking in things that are not*
*there the help he cannot find in those that are, though*
*none can help, since this infinite abyss can be filled only*
*with an infinite and immutable object; in other words*
*by God himself.*[59]

God sent his Son, Jesus, to start to heal wounds and set captives free. In commissioning the ministry of Jesus as he was baptized in the River Jordan, God speaks to the wounds of every human. As the heavens opened the voice of God spoke:

*"You are my beloved Son; with you I am well pleased."*
*(Mark 1:11, ESV)*

How every human being yearns to hear words like this! The great news of the gospel is that God is saying he is delighted with humanity. God is well pleased with us and loves us despite our inadequacies and shame.

God is searching for every human being. In Matthew 13:44, Jesus tells the story of a man who finds a vast treasure in a field. The man covets the treasure and he goes and sells everything he has in order to buy the field. Biblical teaching tells us that this story is about the kingdom of God as the treasure, but it is my own view that this story can be seen as telling about the transforming power of God's grace in a human life; I believe the greater story is that the hidden treasure is you. And me. Because each one of us is the treasure that God gave everything for.

God's relationship with the people of Israel is instructive in the method and manner of God's invitation from generation to generation.

God speaks to Jacob in a dream about the future, and the vision Jacob was given has been repeated over and over again in the years that have followed.

God spoke to Jacob (Israel) in visions of the night and said:

> *"I am God, the God of your father," he said. "Do not be afraid to go down to Egypt, for I will make you into a great nation there. I will go down to Egypt with you, and I will surely bring you back again. And Joseph's own hand will close your eyes." (Genesis 46:3–4)*

In the Christian life we have to go down to a place for a period of testing, but God has promised to bring us back up again. It is in that Egypt-type place of testing, however, that you will be made great. Where is your Egypt? Are you in it right now? Remember God is with you and God will bring you back up again.

This treasure sometimes gets itself into a terrible state. In the time that the children of Israel were in Egypt, a pharaoh arose who did not know Joseph and started to put Joseph's descendants into forced labour. When you forget the promise and the presence of God, you get confused, and so if you don't know who you are you don't have any choice but to work; you can't rest. This may be a forerunner of the workplace stress that we see building and building in our world. The taskmasters of Egypt served a purpose in reminding the children of Israel that they were nothing. They had forgotten that they were God's people. God is inviting his treasured possession into relationship, and yet over and over again, despite the clues to God's presence, we go around blind.

Eventually the cries and prayers of the people are articulated in the actions of the midwives who refuse to kill the baby boys, and Moses is born. But God's invitation is rejected again when Moses kills an Egyptian soldier and flees for his life into the desert.

We rejoin Moses forty years later. God is still inviting him, and this time there is decisive insight. Moses was tending sheep for his father-in-law Jethro when he

> saw that though the bush was on fire it did not burn
> up. So Moses thought, "I will go over and see this
> strange sight – why the bush does not burn up." When
> the Lord saw that he had gone over to look, God called
> to him from within the bush… (Exodus 3:1–4)

At last Moses has taken a second look, and God sees that Moses sees, and then God immediately responds by calling to him. How long had God waited for this moment? It sounds as if God was hoping but not expecting it.

Now look again, focus in, go closer. You might find the missing piece in the jigsaw of life. It happens to all of us. We can be reading a book and all of a sudden a word, or a sentence, or a thought, strikes us. We can be reading a Bible verse that we have read thousands of times, and all of a sudden it comes alive.

*Draw near to God, and he will draw near to you.*
*(James 4:8a, ESV)*

God was planning to invite Pharaoh, who was also afraid, to let the people go, and God was going to do it through Moses. God invited Pharaoh ten times not to be dominated and motivated by fear. Moses accepted the invitation and Pharaoh rejected it. Finally God's invitational promise to Jacob is fulfilled: "I will go down with you to Egypt but bring you back up." God offers that invitation to every human being, but when that call is rejected, God sends for his nearest servant.

Which is where we come in: how can we become inviters for God? When we tune into the call of God in our lives, we find that there are assignments and a calling ready for us from God. We don't choose them; we receive them. Are we going to repress, avoid, resist, or trust the call? Will we be loyal to the call of God, or to our fears? Will we pray and step out in faith?

We feel great resistance to the calling of God at times. We will always feel we don't have what it takes. We might say we are not courageous, not sufficiently educated, lacking the skill set. It is probably true… but callings have an incredible way of growing us. The heroes and their faith journeys often have two initial steps: step one is hearing the call; step two is resisting the call; please see Gideon, Moses, Esther as prime examples!

But as part of the call there is something in it for the inviter. The Bible is full of examples of characters receiving from God a new name – Abram, Jacob, Simon, and Saul to name a few. In the journey of faith they laid down their old identity and started to become who God meant them to be. The story of the angel of the Lord visiting Gideon gives an immediate description of how he was seen by God. Despite threshing wheat in the barn for fear of the Midianites, we remember that the angel addressed him as a "mighty man of valour" (Judges 6:12, ESV).

Moses is full of fear at the burning bush. He starts backing away from God. But he finds that there is nowhere he can run to, as God declares his own name: "I am the God who is always present." Fear recognizes implicitly that there is another and that I am dependent. God says over and over again, "Don't be afraid for I am with you." When you encounter God and pause... there is the beginning of a movement from fear to faith.

Steven Covey, echoing Holocaust survivor Viktor Frankl, wrote:

> *Between stimulus and response there is a space. In*
> *that space lies our freedom and power to choose our*
> *response. In those choices lie our growth and our*
> *happiness.*[60]

We can often experience the stimulus from God as fear, because God is asking us to do something when we are not comfortable. This is why (as we explored earlier) fear should be seen as a gateway into the meaning of life. Many run away and take a pill, but God is knocking at your door. What will you do with this stimulus towards creativity and courage?

Jesus chose twelve apostles from among hundreds of disciples. He gave preferential treatment to three of the twelve. He didn't heal everyone. He didn't feed every hungry crowd. He stopped in the middle of a virtual parade and invited himself over to Zacchaeus's house. Why him? He ensured that strangers would live and allowed Lazarus to die. And what about the incident at the pool of Bethesda? John tells us that Jesus singled out one man among a great number of disabled people... "the blind, the lame, the paralysed" (John 4:3). I don't mean to be critical, but I can't help but imagine Jesus tiptoeing through the crowd saying, "Pardon me, excuse me..." He had clearly received very specific instruction from his Father.

I had never bothered to read the verse that precedes the verse that has guided me for these past five years, "I [Paul] planted ... Apollos watered ... but God has been making it grow." Here it is:

> *the Lord gave opportunity to each one.*
> *(1 Corinthians 3:5, NASB)*

It is God who sends the opportunity to plant an invitation and to nurture a relationship. Let's make sure we develop our prayer life to the level of hearing the nudge or feeling the prompt of God. Reread chapters five and six and pick out some emotional, mental, and physical approaches, and give them a try.

In *missio dei* (the mission of God) God is the primary evangelist. He is the missioner. Yet remarkably God invites us into partnership in that great mission. We are invited on a journey. We can be converts one week and partners in mission the next. Mission is an invitation to get alongside what God is doing.

What is God inviting you to do today?

# Appendix

## Qualitative Measurement for Culture Change

*Quantity of names in unique mission field:*

How many learning partners are reporting results?

How many people are invited?

How many people have accepted?

How many people have rejected?

*Ongoing analysis of the invitation process:*

What types of distorted truth are being reported?

What soul wounds have been identified?

What progress are people reporting on the healing of their wounds?

What are the main reasons for rejection from the people being invited?

What is the ratio of acceptance and rejection?

*Reporting signs of the activity of God in the inviter:*

How did it make you feel?

Did you sense God's love for the person you invited? Or has loving your neighbour been challenged through the experience?

Did you experience joy after you overcame your fear? Or was it an experience that you never want to go through again?

Did you feel peaceful after overcoming your fear of inviting the person?

Are you aware that you are not at peace?

Are you more able to endure rejection? Or are you more aware that this is a difficulty for you?

Will you be more generous by offering more invitations? Or has your generosity been challenged by a refusal?

Are you more devoted to God by the experience? Or has it knocked your faith?

Are you hopeful that the invitation will produce something eventually? Or has it dented your hope?

# Notes

1. Michael Frost and Alan Hirsch, *The Faith of Leap*, Grand Rapids, MI: Baker Books, 2011.

2. Vincent Donovan, *Christianity Rediscovered*, Norwich: SCM Press; new edition, 2001.

3. Stories of Scientific Discovery CUP Archive. http://google.com.au/books?id=Pr88AAAAIAAJ&printsec=frontcover&source=gbs_ge_summary_r&cad=0#v=onepage&q&f=fals (accessed 19.2.15).

4. A number of prominent US sports coaches have used the phrase; it is uncertain when it was first used.

5. Michael Harvey, *Unlocking the Growth*, Oxford: Monarch Books, 2012.

6. Brené Brown, "The Power of Vulnerability", TED talk, www.ted.com/talks (accessed 10.2.15).

7. Alain Botton, *Status Anxiety*, London: Penguin; re-issue edition, 2005.

8. Glynn Harrison, *The Big Ego Trip*, Nottingham: IVP; first edition, 2013.

9. Seth Godin, *The Dip*, London: Piatkus, 2007.

10. Chris Thurman, *The Lies We Tell Ourselves: Overcome lies and experience the emotional health, intimate relationships, and spiritual fulfillment you've been seeking*, Nashville, TN: Thomas Nelson, 1999.

11. Attributed to Mark Twain in *Reader's Digest*, April 1934.

12. Eugene Peterson, *Leap Over a Wall*, San Francisco, CA: HarperSanFrancisco, 2002.

13. Wesley was able to practise what he preached about church discipline because he organized his followers into small groups. A Methodist society included all the Methodists in an area. It was divided into groups, or classes, of twelve. The people met each week

to study the Bible, pray, and report on the state of their souls. Each class had a leader who reported to the preacher in charge of the society. Wesley published a list of questions for the class leaders to help the members examine themselves: 1. What known sins have you committed since our last meeting? 2. What temptations have you overcome? 3. How did God deliver you? 4. What have you thought, said, or done that might be sinful? www.christianhistoryinstitute.org (accessed 11.2.15).

14. *The Confessions of St Augustine* (Book IV, Chapter 12).

15. Leighton Ford, *Good News is for Sharing*, Colorado Springs, CO: David C. Cook, 1977, p. 15.

16. Susan Jeffers, *Feel the Fear and Do it Anyway*, London: Vermilion; twentieth anniversary edition, 2007.

17. Henry David Thoreau, *Walden: or, Life in the Woods*, Charleston, SC: CreateSpace Independent Publishing Platform, 2014.

18. "What Fear Can Teach Us", Ted Talk by Karen Walker, www.ted.com/talks (accessed 11.2.15).

19. "The Quest to Understand Consciousness", Antonio Damasio, www.ted.com/talks (accessed 11.2.15).

20. Northrop Frye, *The Educated Imagination*, Bloomington, IN: Indiana University Press, 1964.

21. These words are displayed over the ark containing the Torah scrolls in many synagogues.

22. C. H. Spurgeon at the Metropolitan Tabernacle, Newington, 2 December 1888.

23. Gordon Neufeld speaking at The Dalai Lama Center (at the Massachusetts Institute of Technology, USA) about "Anxiety in Children and Youth", May 2014.

24. Professor James Pennebaker, "The Secret Life of Pronouns" at TED x Austin http://tedxtalks.ted.com/video/The-Secret-Life-of-Pronouns-J-2 (accessed 19.2.15).

25. Francis Bacon, *The New Organon*, New York, NY: Macmillan USA; facsimile edition, 1960.

26. G. K. Chesterton, *What's Wrong with the World*, Charleston, SC: CreateSpace Independent Publishing Platform, 2009.

27. Richard Rohr, *Breathing Under Water*, Cincinnati, OH: St Anthony Messenger Press, 2011.

28. Walter Brueggemann, quoted in Presbytery of Muskingum Valley Newsletter, news and views, April 1998.

29. Jim Rohn, *7 Strategies for Wealth & Happiness*, Roseville, CA: Prima Life; second edition, 1996.

30. Henry David Thoreau, *Walden, Civil Disobedience and Other Writings* (Norton Critical Editions), New York, NY: W. W. Norton & Company, 3rd revised edition, 2008.

31. Bronnie Ware, *The Top Five Regrets of the Dying*, London: Hay House, 2012.

32. Dennis A. Curyer MA, *7 Ways to Live Life to the Max*, e-book, 2003.

33. Victor and Mildred Goertzel, *Cradles of Eminence*, New York, NY: Little, Brown & Company, 1962.

34. Brené Brown, "Listening to Shame", TED talk, www.ted.com/talk (accessed 12.2.15).

35. G. K. Chesterton, *Orthodoxy*, Charleston, SC: CreateSpace Independent Publishing Platform, 2012.

36. Beverley Shepherd, *Insight into Stress*, Surrey: CWR, 2006.

37. http://rescomp.stanford.edu/~cheshire/EinsteinQuotes.html (accessed 12.2.15).

38. Brendon Burchard, *The Charge*, London: Simon & Schuster Ltd, 2012.

39. William Shakespeare, *The Tragedy of Julius Caesar*, believed to have been written in 1599.

40. Franklin D. Roosevelt, first inauguration speech as the thirty-second President of the United States in March 1933.

41. Will Smith YouTube video of Inspirational Words of Wisdom.

42. http://sethgodin.typepad.com/seths_blog/2013/12/important-nervous.html (accessed 12.2.15).

43.  Jonathan Fields, *Uncertainty*, London: Penguin; reprint edition, 2013.

44.  Yann Martel, *The Life of Pi*, Edinburgh, Canongate Books Ltd; film tie-in edition, 2012.

45.  Kelly McGonigal, "How to Make Stress Your Friend", TED Global 2013, www.ted.com/talks (accessed 12.2.15).

46.  Adapted from Genesis 12:1.

47.  Rollo May, *The Courage to Create*, W. W. Norton & Company; new edition, 1994.

48.  Seth Godin, *Purple Cow*, London: Penguin, 2005.

49.  Beverley Shepherd, *Insight into Stress*, Surrey: CWR, 2006.

50.  Eugene H. Peterson, *Under the Unpredictable Plant*, Grand Rapids, MI: William B. Eerdmans Publishing Co, 1996.

51.  Quote from T. S. Eliot (1888–1965).

52.  This is part of the text of the Commencement Address delivered by Steve Jobs, CEO of Apple Computer and of Pixar Animation Studios, on 12 June 2005.

53.  Fritz Perls, MD, psychiatrist and founder of gestalt therapy.

54.  Michael Jordan, Nike commercial.

55.  Alan Redpath, *Victorious Christian Living*, Charleston, SC: CreateSpace Independent Publishing Platform, 2013.

56.  Daniel Kahneman, *Thinking, Fast and Slow*, London: Penguin, 2012.

57.  Alan Hirsh and Michael Frost, Baker Books (15 April 2011).

58.  Rudolph Otto, *The Idea of the Holy*, Oxford: Oxford University Press, second edition, 1958.

59.  Thomas V. Morris, *Making Sense of it All: Pascal and the Meaning of Life*, Grand Rapids, MI: William B. Eerdmans Publishing Co, 1959.

60.  Steven Covey, *The 7 Habits of Highly Effective People*, London: Simon & Schuster Ltd; reprinted edition, 2004.